THE BLACK IN CRIMSON AND BLACK

HISTORY AND PROFILES OF AFRICAN AMERICANS AT SDSU

By Robert Fikes, Jr., Librarian
San Diego State University
Library and Information Access
2019

Published by
Montezuma Publishing
Aztec Shops Ltd.
San Diego State University
San Diego, California 92182-1701
619-594-7552

www.montezumapublishing.com

Copyright © 2019
All Rights Reserved.

ISBN: 978-1-7269-0085-0

Copyright © 2019 by author Robert Fikes Jr. The compilation, formatting, printing and binding of this work is the exclusive copyright of Montezuma Publishing and the author Robert Fikes Jr. All rights reserved. No part of this work may be reproduced, stored in a retrieval system, or transmitted in any form or by any means, including digital, except as may be expressly permitted by the applicable copyright statutes or with written permission of the Publisher or Author.

Publishing Manager: Lia Dearborn
Cover Design: Angelica Lopez
Design, Layout, and Formatting : Angelica Lopez

CONTENTS

FOREWORD 5

THE EARLY YEARS, 1907-1929 7

THE 1930'S 13

THE 1940'S 21

THE 1950'S 33

THE 1960'S 47

THE 1970'S 67

THE 1980'S 99

THE 1990'S 127

THE 21 ST CENTURY 157

NOTES 189

ADDENDUM A:
SELECTED PUBLICATION BY BLACK SDSU FACULTY AND STAFF 193

ADDENDUM B:
SDSU AWARDS TO AFRICAN AMERICAN FACULTY, STAFF, AND ALUMNI 201

INDEX 203

FOREWORD

The history of African Americans at San Diego State offers a look at the best and the brightest, from all over the country, decade after decade. Why were African American scholars drawn to San Diego State knowing they would represent a very small minority of those on campus? We believe that this collection of profiles will help to answer that question.

Inside the pages of *The Black and Crimson: History and Profiles of African Americans at SDSU*, you will see a brief biography of each person's credentials, as they were when they started at SDSU. If you know those featured, or if you research them, you will find these scholars have accomplished so much, and reached unexpected heights in their fields of study. The success of our predecessors are part of the reason why African American's in academia continue to accept positions SDSU. While never an easy road, SDSU has offered and continues to offer opportunities in which African Americans excel, exceed their potential, and in turn put SDSU on the national stage. Robert Fikes, Jr. retired SDSU Librarian, has provided this wonderful compilation and at his request, proceeds will benefit the Henrietta Goodwin Scholars Program and The Black Resource Center on campus. We apologize in advance for any unintentional omissions.

My hope for you after reading this book is that you will carry the pride provided by those who came before you. I hope you are inspired and motivated to reach new heights. After all, this collection of profiles is proof that you can achieve your dreams with the foundation you will receive at San Diego State University.

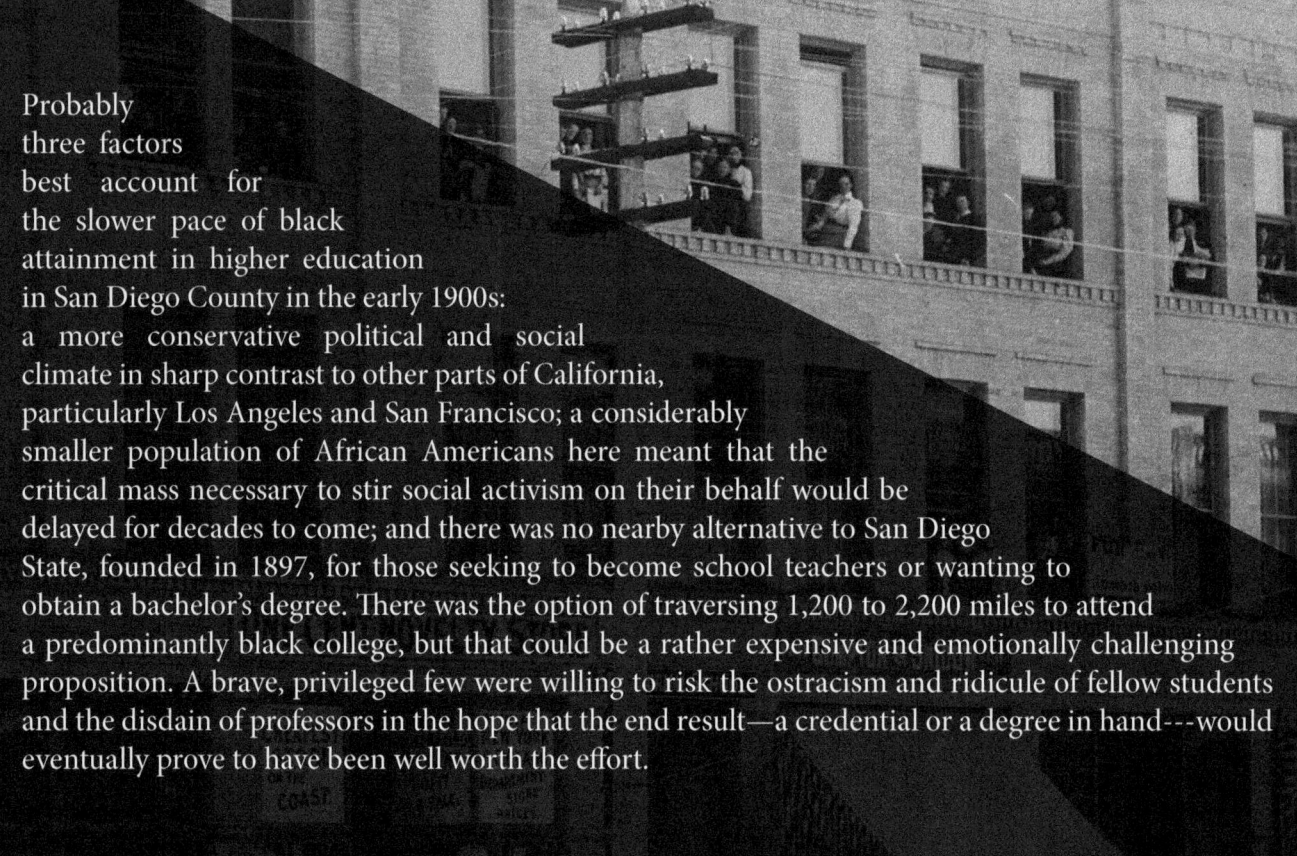

Probably
three factors
best account for
the slower pace of black
attainment in higher education
in San Diego County in the early 1900s:
a more conservative political and social
climate in sharp contrast to other parts of California,
particularly Los Angeles and San Francisco; a considerably
smaller population of African Americans here meant that the
critical mass necessary to stir social activism on their behalf would be
delayed for decades to come; and there was no nearby alternative to San Diego
State, founded in 1897, for those seeking to become school teachers or wanting to
obtain a bachelor's degree. There was the option of traversing 1,200 to 2,200 miles to attend
a predominantly black college, but that could be a rather expensive and emotionally challenging
proposition. A brave, privileged few were willing to risk the ostracism and ridicule of fellow students
and the disdain of professors in the hope that the end result—a credential or a degree in hand---would
eventually prove to have been well worth the effort.

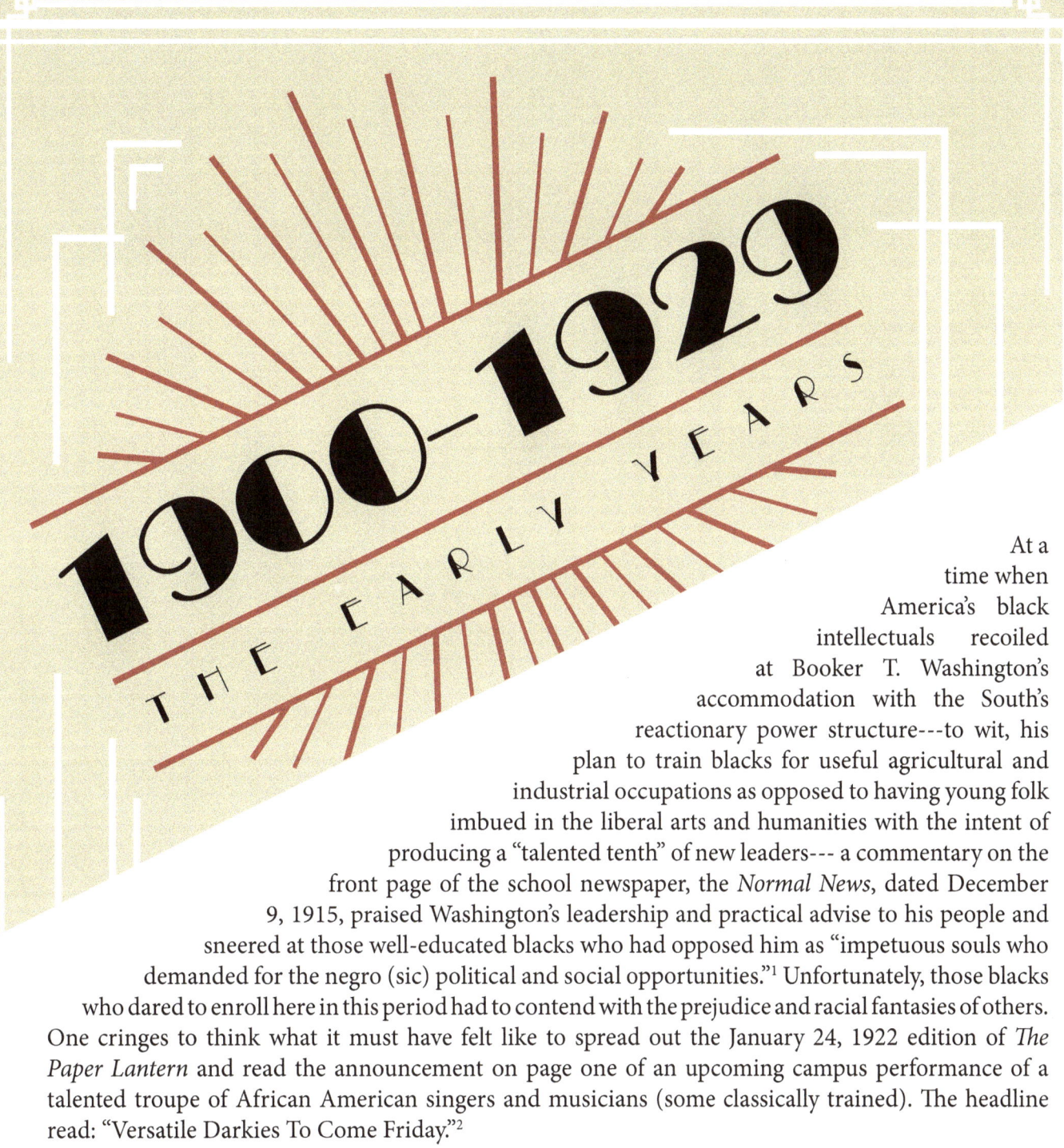

1900-1929
THE EARLY YEARS

At a time when America's black intellectuals recoiled at Booker T. Washington's accommodation with the South's reactionary power structure---to wit, his plan to train blacks for useful agricultural and industrial occupations as opposed to having young folk imbued in the liberal arts and humanities with the intent of producing a "talented tenth" of new leaders--- a commentary on the front page of the school newspaper, the *Normal News*, dated December 9, 1915, praised Washington's leadership and practical advise to his people and sneered at those well-educated blacks who had opposed him as "impetuous souls who demanded for the negro (sic) political and social opportunities."[1] Unfortunately, those blacks who dared to enroll here in this period had to contend with the prejudice and racial fantasies of others. One cringes to think what it must have felt like to spread out the January 24, 1922 edition of *The Paper Lantern* and read the announcement on page one of an upcoming campus performance of a talented troupe of African American singers and musicians (some classically trained). The headline read: "Versatile Darkies To Come Friday."[2]

The Goodwin Sisters: The Lonely Pioneers

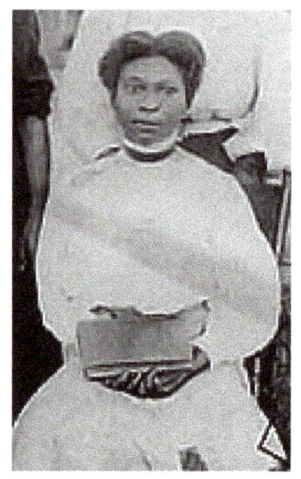

It was a clear, crisp and typically mild winter's day on January 30, 1913 when 15 graduates turned out for the commencement ceremony of San Diego Normal School, then a place where mostly females finished a two-year curriculum to become teachers. Strangely, the *San Diego Union* failed to mention Henrietta Goodwin (left) in its list of the 15 graduates, nor did the school list her on its roster of graduates. However, both an attendance ledger and her registration record card indicate that she did in fact graduate on January 30, 1913, having attended the school sporadically since 1908.[3] Goodwin's sizeable family, of whom all of the adults could read and write, had left Forth Worth, Texas hoping for a better life in San Diego.[4]

It was her younger sister, Lela (right), who had first tried to succeed here and preceded Henrietta as a registered student in 1907, but she dropped out after taking just four classes. The Goodwin sisters worked occasionally as domestic servants to support their studies. They both entertained a rather impossible dream: to work in the public school system which at the time forbade African Americans teachers as full-time permanent employees. The best they could hope for was part-time work. Henrietta Goodwin, our first African American graduate, soon left the county but other ambitious black women persisted. According to a surviving relative, Dr. Beverly Goodwin at Indiana University at Pennsylvania, the Goodwin sisters died during an epidemic, probably before 1925.

Ruby Berkley Goodwin: Renaissance Woman

By 1922, the school had doubled its size to nearly 470 students and had officially been renamed San Diego State Teachers College. That same year Ruby Carmen Berkley (1903-1961)---better known by her married name, Ruby Berkley Goodwin (sister-in-law of Henrietta and Leah Goodwin of the above)---completed coursework for a teaching certification and returned home to Imperial Valley to teach in El Centro, marry, and start a family. She later attended Fullerton Junior College. What seemed like the beginning of a respectable career in education took a detour into notoriety after her attempts to become a published author resulted in some literary sketches of African American life that were used in composer William Grant Still's *Negro Spirituals* (1949).[5] What followed were essays and lectures; two books of poetry; and an autobiography recalling her childhood years in Illinois, titled *It's Good To Be Black*,[6] which won the gold medal from the Commonwealth Club for the best nonfiction book by a California author in 1953 and set to be republished in 2012. From 1936 to 1952 Ruby was

personal secretary and publicist for actress Hattie McDaniel. She had her own stage and screen career, wrote a syndicated column for black newspapers called "Hollywood in Bronze," and was honored as the first black named California State Mother of the Year in 1955---all from an alumnus who once sang in the school's glee club and who was the second black to complete a course of study here.

In
t h e
1 9 3 0 s
people were
mostly referring to
the school as San Diego State
College (not its official name) and the
school colors had changed from white and
gold to crimson and black. Now a four-year degree
granting co-ed institution, its Park Boulevard location
was bursting at the seams with an enrollment of 1,250 students
while administrators prepared to move the campus to Montezuma
Mesa six miles to the east.[7] For African Americans, the decade got off to an
auspicious beginning when Minnie Lee Brown obtained her elementary teaching
credential and appeared in cap and gown in the 1930 student yearbook.

In scanning student newspapers between 1913 and 1939 (the *Normal News Weekly*, *The Paper Lantern*, the *State College Aztec*, and *The Aztec*) one can easily detect a certain ambivalence regarding blacks on campus and blacks generally. There was no apparent hostility direct at them. There were flattering reviews of books by black authors and concerts by black entertainers passing through the area; and lectures and speeches on the state of blacks, sometimes featuring local black community leaders, were mentioned or publicized. Take for example the brief announcement in April 1938 headlined "Negro Education Will Be Subject of Address" which read: "Reverend Hampton of the Bethel Baptist church has been asked to speak at the next meeting of the Roger Williams club. His subject will deal with the advancement of higher education among Negro young people. Special music will be provided by the colored church."[8] In the late 1920s there was a profile of Paul Robeson that was quite positive in tone.

1930's

In 1936, an editorial recognized the growing independence of black voters; and another editorial in 1936 was in support of a court decision in Georgia reversing the conviction of black labor organizer Angela Herndon who had been sentenced to 18-20 years on the chain gain. On the surface there did not seem to be any greater problem here with racial prejudice and discriminatory treatment than any other college in the state.

On the other hand, in this period blacks were too few in number to attract much attention. In 1937, there were roughly 25 of them out of a total student enrollment of nearly 1,700. Conscious of their role as representative of a small but growing racial community in the city, they conducted themselves as perfect ladies and gentlemen, never giving their white fellow students, professors and administrators the slightest cause for alarm. Still, one cannot help but to notice that in group photos in the yearbooks blacks invariable are positioned in the rear or at the end of a row of people as if they were not fully accepted by the group. And though service

The Woodsonians (1938)

and pre-professional organizations were open to them, being rushed by Greek letter sororities and fraternities—groups that dominated important aspects of student life—was out of the question.

Blossom Lorraine Van Lowe-Gholston: Fullfilling a Dream

In 1933, San Francisco native Blossom Lorraine Van Lowe-Gholston graduated with an A.B. degree. A co-founder of the Woodsonians, a group named after black historian Carter G. Woodson which served as a safe haven for black students to socialize and discuss issues of the day, Van Lowe-Gholston later would become a charter member and president of the local chapter of Delta Sigma Theta Sorority. More significant, she achieved the long-cherished goal of educated blacks: that of being hired as a regular school teacher at a San Diego City public school. This was accomplished on July 21, 1942 when, after earning a master's degree at Columbia University, and because of the agitation of local black activists, she began teaching at Memorial Junior High where she had earlier been a pupil.[9] Van Lowe-Gholston's achievement as the city's first black teacher has to be seen in the context of a region stubbornly resistant to social change. Contrast the odyssey of black would-be teachers in San Diego to that of their counterparts 124 miles north of here. Bessie Bruington Burke received her teaching credential at the Los Angeles State Normal School (later absorbed by UCLA) in 1911 and soon thereafter became the first black public school teacher in Los Angeles. By 1918 she was a school Principal in a more liberal region of Southern California.

Bessie Alberta Cobb: Positive Attitude Personified

Regardless if African Americans were invited or welcomed to join student groups there were some individuals who were determined to force them to integrate their ranks. One such intrepid soul was Bessie A. Cobb (Class of '39) who was a member of the College YWCA; Gamma Psi literary honor society; Amotl, a group fostering future librarians; the foreign language honor society Alpha Mu Gamma; and, of course, the Woodsonians. An English major, Cobb received a $50 scholarship from the NAACP. She contributed a poem titled "Beauty" and an essay, "If I Could Choose," to the popular student literary journal, *El Palenque*. In the 1938 essay she pondered what she might decide if she could choose her nationality, race, sex, and parentage. She concluded with this memorable statement of pride and self-affirmation:

> Is it surprising that in such a country one should have to be careful about the choice of her color? Nevertheless, it is true. To be dark-skinned as I am now is to fill one's path with obstacles....I choose to remain a Negro. I cannot give up my people. What should I do without their patience and their sympathy, their simple, age-old wisdom, their rich song, and their warm living beauty....No, I would not be anything else in the world. It is a call, a challenge, and if I can reach the goal of my dream, so much greater the achievement. It is worth it, every bit....So I have lost my four wishes, because I do not

wish to be anyone else in the world but myself. That is really what I have chosen, for a change in any one of the factors of race, nationality, sex, or parentage would have made me a different person. It is my dream, and I shall have to fulfill it. I am content. I am pleased to be myself.[10]

Cobb's assuredness and optimism served her well. She went on to earn a master's degree at Atlanta University and worked as a homemaker and freelance writer. Another startling fact about Cobb was that her poem "Change," along with four poems by black alumna Ruby Goodwin, was published in the classic anthology *Negro Voices* (1938) that included works by soon to be literary giants Langston Hughes, Nick Aaron Ford, and Melvin Tolson. Essentially, this establishes that San Diego State produced two of the most promising young black poets in the pre-World War II era.

Jonathan T. Buchanan: Intelligence and Ambition

Just as confident and perhaps with even more drive was the bespectacled Jonathan T. Buchanan (Class of '36), the first black male to graduate at San Diego State. Described in the 1931 San Diego City Directory as a laborer, Buchanan had been an elder and, briefly, the leader of the Beacon Light Seventh Day Adventist Church.[11] A zoology major, he left the city to pursue a career in health care. By 1949 he was advertising in the *Los Angeles Sentinel* his "GRAND, NEW and very BEAUTIFUL ULTRA-MODERN OFFICES" at 4350 Avalon Blvd.[12] He was by then Dr. Jonathan T. Buchanan, an optometrist offering eye examinations, prescription glasses and vision training using equipment that was, "SCIENTIFIC and SUPER DELUXE and said by those who KNOW to surpass all others in Southern California."[13]

Thelma Gorham Thompson: Eloquence and Purpose

In those rare cases in which a black student was mentioned in the student newspaper their race was almost never called attention to, even when the topic or event had something specifically to do with them. Thelma Gorham Thompson (Class of '37) participated in more extracurricular activities than any other African American student, including Cap & Gown and the Toastmistresses Club. On November 10, 1936, Gorham was announced inconspicuously as one of the main speakers for the Armistice Day celebration. She told an assembly of students that they "should cultivate an atmosphere of peace within themselves and try to transmit it to others."[14] A gifted public speaker, she later moved to Chicago, retired as chief of the U.S Department of Health and Human Resources Children's Bureau, Region V, and was honored for her leadership in planning adoptions of minority children.[15] She co-authored the book *Adoptive Resources for Negro Children* (New York: Child Welfare League, 1959). She retired to San Francisco.

Robert Clinton Moss: A Legacy Beyond Athletics

The first black student to appear in a photo in the student newspaper was Robert C. "Jo Jo" Moss (1914-2008), the school's first black sports star and the first black to play on an athletic team. In addition to playing football, Moss was named "the most valuable man" by his varsity basketball teammates in 1935 (winner of the Paul W. Mott Basketball Trophy) and was twice all-conference leading scorer. A group photo of the team in the 1934 yearbook has Moss, the only black on the team, in a row of players along with the future star entertainer Art Linkletter. In the early 1940s he was appointed the first black U.S. Post Office supervisor in San Diego and later became president of the San Diego branch of the National Alliance of Postal and Federal Employees. In the late1940s, Moss help found the Paramount Golf Club because blacks then were excluded from membership in white clubs.[16] He could boast that both his son Robert C. Moss Jr. (Class of '61) who was a professional baseball umpire and who taught physical education at UCSD, and grandson Parry Moss (Class of '94) graduated from San Diego State.

Clarence Hilayer King Jr.: Management Pioneer

From 1934 to 1935 future engineer Clarence King (1915-1996) attended San Diego State. He was one of two blacks who was active in the Aztec chapter of University Bible Clubs. He transferred to the University of Southern California where he graduated in 1944. Prior to military service in World War II he worked at Ratner Manufacturing and Vultee Aircraft in San Diego. In Los Angeles he worked for twenty years as manager of data processing for Golden State Mutual, as project administrator for Rockwell International for six years, then as a management consultant. Clarence served as international president of the Association for Systems Management and was twice listed in *Who's Who in the West*. He died in Los Angeles 1996.

There were two more standouts in the 1930s. Henry G. Manley Sr. (Class of '37) who was on the track team rose to the rank of Major in the U.S. Army. After retirement he became president of the San Diego Track and Field Officials Association. And the always dapper Dr. Horace Mays (Class of '37), who was a member of the Aztec University Bible Club, became executive director of the Los Angeles Council of Churches and once lead a seminar on "Racial Problems and the Local Church" in conjunction with a 1963 Billy Graham Crusade.

On December 7, 1940, a crowd of 1200 packed the Aztec gymnasium to see in person Jackie Robinson, the star on the UCLA basketball squad. At the time Robinson was considered the best all-around athlete in the nation, playing on several sports teams at UCLA. Of course, this event was far overshadowed exactly a year later when the Japanese attacked Pearl Harbor. Some of the school's finest students would bravely serve and die in a global struggle that simply had to be won. College students were more likely to become officers in the military which needed the brightest and most capable young leaders to run the machinery of war, including black men like Nelson F. Pallemon Sr. (Class of '40) who served his country as an Army First Lieutenant.

The 1940 U.S. Census recorded 4,143 African American residents (2%) in the city of San Diego. In contrast, there were 63,774 blacks living in Los Angeles. San Diego's blacks were ordinarily mistreated by whites who discriminated against them using restrictive covenants in property deeds; denied access to certain public accommodations like the once prestigious U.S. Grant Hotel; and the most educated of them were customarily assigned as maids, janitors, and porters. To add insult to injury, black San Diegans were also viewed by blacks in other parts of the country as not quite worthy of attention. Not one of the 400 persons profiled in the monumental 1928-1929 edition of *Who's Who in Colored America* lived in San Diego. And equally galling to some, not a single black San Diegan was mentioned in the 1948 edition of *Negro Who's Who in California*.[17] The perception that the city was distant and well off the beaten path meant that some very talented people here would not get the national exposure they deserved from the black press.

1940's

Perusing issues of the school newspaper one can trace the rise of race consciousness and efforts to improve race relations on and off campus. The main impetus for this was the overarching event of the decade: World War II. The global conflict forced humanity to face the horrifying results of totalitarianism and pseudo-scientific racial theories that set the stage for atrocities against various ethnic groups. In this country the signal contribution of patriotic African Americans to the war effort, coupled with their growing sense of empowerment, meant that they would increasingly resist the kind of mistreatment they had endured for so long.

Six months before the attack on Pearl Harbor a campus "Y committee" investigating racial prejudice in employment in San Diego found that, "not a single Negro (was) employed in the defense industries higher than that of a sweeper or janitor."[18] But the committee members did not have to look any further than the student newspaper to find evidence of racial prejudice. In the Op/Ed section of the April 29, 1941 issue of *The Aztec* a cartoon featured a black African with bloated white lips and human bones scattered near his feet listening to a message sent via talking drums that said "Bokidy Boom Thud." The caption read: "Say, dat new announcer sho don't enunciate clearly."[19] They were painfully reminded of their otherness, as was the case in the 1942 school yearbook which had beneath the photo of a mound of football players the caption "Nigger Pile."[20] More subtle but quite revealing is a 1942 yearbook photo of YWCA members[21] which had black student Willamay Kennedy (Class of '45) isolated, off to the far left edge of the scene pretending to admire a flower arrangement while pairs of other members (all white) are turned towards each other presumably discussing matters of relevance to the organization. Implicit in this and other similarly staged photos in which there was one or two blacks is that their participation in majority white groups—like their presence on this majority white campus—was hardly a welcomed or ordinary event. Understandably, fearing they would be socially marginalized and harassed because of their race is largely what persuaded promising high school graduates in the region to consider the alternative of attending faraway historically black colleges.

1947 Ivy Leaf Club

Through the years there have been sympathetic white SDSU faculty members willing to go the extra mile to personally encourage minority race students and defend the notion of a racially diverse campus. Three such professors in the 1940s were anthropologist Spencer Rogers, sociologist Kenneth Barnhart, and, most notably, the popular and revered psychologist Harry C. Steinmetz who was later persecuted during the anti-Communist witch-hunting McCarthy era and eventually found work at Morehouse College. In the spring of 1944, at the request of black students and other interested parties, all three professors reviewed the pamphlet "The Races of Mankind," authored by Columbia University anthropologist Ruth Benedict, which had been withdrawn from circulation in the Army and the USO because of a southern Congressman's found it message of racial egalitarianism objectionable. The professors endorsed the pamphlet and announced that the information contained therein was scientifically sound and "factually verifiable."[22]

THE 1940'S

There were other indications during the post-war years that race relations had entered a new phase consistent with changes in American society. In 1948, a play titled "Black and White," written by Frederic Fishman, the student managing editor of *The Aztec*, concerning "the circumstance brought about by the entrance of a negro (sic) soldier into the sick bay of an American-bound hospital ship,"[23] won first place in the Annual One-Act Play Tournament. In 1949, members of the Jewish organization Hillel and the InterFaith Council promoted a new group called the Inter-Cultural Organization whose goal was to foster better race relations. Japanese nationals and Japanese Americans, noticeably absent in the yearbooks of the war years, were returning to campus. Also, racially insensitive cartoons like the often repeated image of Monty Montezuma holding a tomahawk in one hand and a blood-dripping scalp of an Aztec opponent in the other hand (one gory drawing had Monty cutting out a heart from a body) vanished from the sports section of the student newspaper. Still, there were obvious signs of entrenched resistance. In the spring of 1948 the student body voted 1255 to 771 to defeat an anti-discrimination measure brought before it by way of a petition signed by 400 concerned students.[24] The measure was thought to have posed a threat to the social sororities and fraternities unwilling as ever to end their long tradition of selective exclusion.

Orlando Coons: America's First Black Champion Gymnast

A prime example of an outstanding local black overlooked by the national media and the black press is the case of Orlando Coons (1915-1998), the unheralded first African America to successfully complete as a gymnast at the national level. Coons enrolled as a student in 1936 and was on the track team (pole vault and hurdles) when the beloved coach C. E. Peterson noticed him working out on the high bar and decided to sign up the young man for a gymnastics contest. Representing San Diego State College, Coons was picked all-round champion at the 1939 and 1940 California College Athletic Association Championships. In 1945, he was all-round champion in gymnastics in the Amateur Athletic Union (AAU) Southern Pacific section; in 1950, he finished sixth in national all-round competition and was given a berth on the U.S. National Team; and, amazingly in his last national competition at age 45 he placed 13th at the AAU meet in 1961.

Peterson thought so highly of Coons that he hired him as coach of the school's gymnastics team during the war years, thus likely becoming the first black gymnastics coach at a predominantly white college or university. A severed big toe suffered in an accident as a child and the resulting foot deformity kept him out of military service but his volunteer work in the community spanned decades, most notably his efforts to teach kids gymnastics at area YMCAs. Coons left San Diego to complete his bachelor's degree in engineering at UC Berkeley but returned here to work for 37 years at the North Island Naval Air Station. Two of his sons graduated from SDSU: Orlando "Skip" Coons (Class of '77), an outstanding high school football coach who lives in Poway; and Steven L. Coons (Class of '73), a professor at San Diego Miramar College. Regrettably, to this day the achievements of Coons as a pioneering black gymnast and coach are not to be found in widely distributed reference books by sports writers and sports historians, including those that focus on black athletes.[25] The man who was once considered the best all-round gymnast on the west coast deserves far more recognition.

The Talented Lipscomb Brothers: Wendell, Airman-Doctor; Ira, Super Student; Olin, Athlete

Another example—one that the campus and city's print media could have played up—is that of Wendell Lipscomb and his brothers. One of the least known facts about the school's African American alumni is that one of them, Wendell Ralph Lipscomb, belonged to the famed Tuskegee Airmen. And he wasn't just your ordinary famed Tuskegee airmen because he actually trained them. Wendell attended San Diego State in the early '40s before World War II began. His education here was cut short because of military service. Along with the best and brightest of his generation, he was sent to Tuskegee to train to fly military planes which was also an experiment to prove whether blacks were as capable as whites of handling the complexities of flying. Wendell wound up a pilot instructor. In the book *A-Train: Memoirs of a Tuskegee Airman* (1997) by Charles W. Dryden, a group photo shows Lipscomb with other instructors. He is seen wearing aviation goggles and a leather jacket. Wendell R. Lipscomb He is kneeling in front of the young Daniel "Chappie" James, later the nation's first Black four-star general.[26] Some of the feats of the legendary Tuskegee airman were unprecedented. They were renowned for their highly successful and heroic defense of Allied bombers, the destruction and disabling of the earliest German jet fighters, and the sinking of a German destroyer by via staffing. After the war, Wendell returned here to get his bachelor's degree in zoology "with distinction" (as did Roy Eldridge Logan in education) in 1947. After obtaining his medical degree at UC Berkeley, Wendell did a three-year stint in the U.S. Air Force as a psychiatrist. With the help of the Black newspaper

Wendell R. Lipscomb

publisher Carlton Goodlett he became the first black to intern at a Kaiser Permanente hospital in San Francisco. He worked at several hospitals and was employed by private and governmental agencies in Northern California.

Ira H. Lipscomb

Wendell worked for quite a while in the state's public heath department. In 1959 he founded the Alcohol Research Group which is still active. He died in a traffic accident in San Francisco in 2004. Wendell's two brothers, Ira Hamilton Lipscomb and Olin Kenneth Lipscomb, also attended school here in the 1940s. Ira appears prominently--getting more attention than any student--in the 1942 yearbook. There are three photos of him: one of him posing as the editor of the 1940-1941 *Student Hand Book*; one of him as an actor in a play; and one of him posing as a lecturer with a caption indicating that he was associate editor of *El Palenque*, active in Skull & Dagger, a student council appointee, listed in *National Collegiate Who's Who*, etc. A member of the Theater Guild and the Radio Workshop, he also contributed articles on campus life to the *The Aztec*. To finance his education Ira worked part-time as a janitor and as a drug store clerk. When the war ended Ira moved to Los Angeles, became a reading consultant for the Los Angeles Unified School District, and died there died in 1991. Brother Olin, who was on the freshman basketball team in 1941, supported the war effort in Italy as a Staff Sergeant crew chief servicing P-47 and B-25 aircraft for the 332nd Fighter Group (Tuskegee Airmen). He died in Los Angeles in 1995.

Olin Lipscomb

John Ritchey: State's Version of Jackie Robinson

A native San Diegan, John Ritchey's career in baseball began when he was a boy playing for the Post #6 American League Team which won two national championships (he was held back from participating in a championship game after smacking two home runs during batting practice).[27] He played outstanding ball for the Aztecs in the years preceding and following World War II but was snubbed by the pro scouts who were only interested in signing up his white teammates. However, Ritchey, the only black on the 1946 Aztec team, found work in the Negro American League and batted an amazing .369 in 1947 to lead the NAL.[28] Popular with the hometown baseball fans, he signed with the San Diego Padres in 1948 and, a la Jackie Robinson in the major leagues a year earlier, Ritchey broke the color barrier in the Pacific Coast League.[29] He withstood the indifference of teammates and the bad sportsmanship of opposing team players who, in the end, failed to curb his sizzling performance. Playing for Vancouver in 1951 he was picked as Player of the Year and batted .343. He died January 17, 2003 and is honored with a bronze bust (left) displayed at Petco Park.

The Hubert Sisters: Maintaining a Proud Family Tradition

We know quite a bit about the Hubert clan because Ruby L. Hubert and her sister Clarice Hubert Simon co-wrote a 222-page family history in 1985 titled *A Century of Black Princes: A Family Tree*.[30] Ruby and Clarice both graduated with degrees in elementary education in 1942. By the late 1940s Ruby was teaching in the public school system. She eventually ran the Neighborhood House Association serving San Diego's underprivileged citizens. Clarice was active in several student groups including the Dance Guild (she starred in Clarice (seated) in "Admetus" the annual school play, "Admetus"), published a short story in *El Palenque*, and was president of the all-black Ivy League Club, a pledge group for Alpha Kappa Alpha Sorority. She became a teacher and junior high principal at three schools in the Los Angeles (Berendo, Dodson, and Henry Clay). Clarice earned her doctorate in education at UCLA in 1980. Both sisters died in Southern California in 2001.

Willie Samuel Steele: Olympic Gold Medalist

It is probably safe to state that no Aztec athlete was as roundly praised and honored during his collegiate career as Willie S. Steele, and deservedly so. The tall, stoic, pillar of inner strength proved to be a public relations dream come true. A stellar track star and graduate of San Diego's Hoover High School, in the post-war years at San Diego State Steele bagged two NCAA titles (1947 and 1948) and won three national AAU championships in his specialty, the long jump. He also played on Aztec basketball and baseball teams. These accomplishments, however, pale in comparison to his winning an Olympic gold medal in London in 1948 with a jump of 7.82 meters (25 feet 8 inches). It was the first ever Olympic medal for an Aztec athlete and the school showed its appreciation accordingly. The 1949 yearbook was dedicated to Steele, followed by a full-page mug shot. He was installed as the first African American member of the Blue Key service fraternity whose national convention had recently removed a race restriction clause from its charter. An editorial in *The Aztec*, February 3, 1949, further underscored Steele's legacy:

> Willie Steele did not have to go to San Diego State, but he chose to do so. He carried the school name into the Olympic news releases….But Willie has gone on giving service to the school. Business clubs around San Diego demanded the Olympic champion for luncheon and dinner speeches, and Willie consented to speak. But the business men found something more than an athlete. They discovered they liked his soft, unassuming way of speaking, and that Willie is one of the best good-will ambassadors that the college has had in a long time. Willie has made numerous appearances at various high schools around the city, working at the job of selling State College to students, and a lot of them have been sold….In the larger picture Willie is aiding in the improvement of race relations. Those who know him respect him as a champion, and think of him as a gentleman.[31]

Steele was elected to the Hall of Champions in Balboa Park in 1958. On September 19, 1989 he died of cancer in Oakland, California where he had worked for many years in the city's Parks and Recreation Department.

The Competitive Henson Brothers: Harold T. Henson and Allison M. Henson Jr.

Aside from the fact that both of the Henson brothers were on the same San Diego State wrestling team in the late 1940s, that both were military wrestling champions, and that both achieved the rank of Army colonel serving with distinction in three major wars, their careers took rather surprising but successful paths when they both retired from military service in 1970. Their African American father

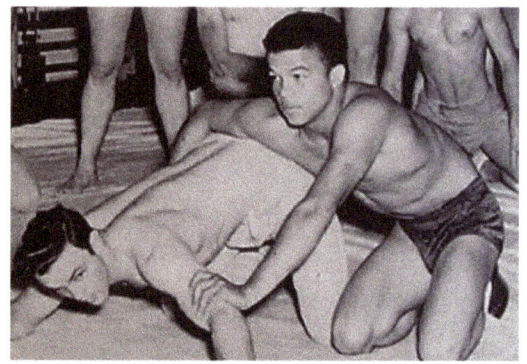

Harold T. Henson, 1942

and Native American mother had moved the family from Oklahoma's Choctaw reservation to San Diego during the Great Depression. In 1941 Harold (Class of '50) entered San Diego State and, encouraged by older brother Allison, became a member of the wrestling team. With the onset of World War II Harold left campus to join the Army. In 1946 he was a European Area Army wrestling champion. He returned to campus in the late 1940s and, according to sports writer Mark Palmer, made sports history as the first African American ever to compete at the national level: at the 1949 NCAA Wrestling Championships held at Colorado State University.

Harold reentered the Army and served in Korea where he earned the Bronze Star. He retired from the military with the Legion of Merit medal. Back in civilian life he worked for 21 years for the city of Washington, D.C., rising to Deputy Director of Public Works.

Brother Allison (left) was in the Army Corps of Engineers during WWII. He returned to San Diego State in the late Harold T. Henson 1940s, served in the Army during wars in Korea and Vietnam and earned both the Purple Heart and Bronze Star. Upon leaving the Army he was awarded a doctorate at the National College of Chiropractic in Illinois and practiced his profession until his death in 1986 in Alexandria, Virginia, the city where brother Harold and his wife still reside.

Harold T. Henson

Benjamin Wallace Cloud

In the book *Black Sailor, White Navy* (2007) by John D. Sherwood, El Cajon native Benjamin W. Cloud is credited with almost single-handedly diffusing a race riot aboard the powerful aircraft carrier USS Kitty Hawk, perhaps the most frightening in a series of violent racial incidents that occurred on numerous ships throughout the fleet during the latter years of the Vietnam War. Born in 1931, the son of San Diego's first black policeman, as a teenager Cloud played violin in the California Youth Symphony. From 1949 to 1952 he attended SDSU, winning a $50 first place prize in the annual engineering student essay contest that merited mention and his photo in *The Aztec* (photo right). The Korean War cut short his studies but he eventually was awarded a bachelor's degree at the University of Maryland and a master's degree in foreign relations at George Washington University. Cloud trained to become a Navy pilot and flew jets like the F8U Crusader and the RA-5

(photo left), earning the Air Medal and Distinguished Flying Cross. In 1966 he became the first black to serve as a White House military social aide. A top graduate of his Naval War College class, in August 1972 Cloud made history again as the first African American Executive Officer of the Kitty Hawk, just in time to put himself directly in harms way when random violence broke out on October 12. He told angry, rampaging blacks, "For the first time you have a 'brother' who is the Executive Officer," then later faced down a group of 150 armed whites intent on retaliating. But his calm, decisive action that day was not fully appreciated or rewarded by the Navy. Later, Cloud directed the NROTC program at Prairie View A&M University and commanded U.S. Naval Support Activity in Naples, Italy. After retiring as a captain in 1984 he was involved in local real estate development and for many years was a board member of the San Diego Air & Space Museum.

George Mitchell Coleman

Growing up in a "multicultural enclave" of La Jolla, George M. Coleman learned to speak Spanish and became an avid cyclist, woodcarver, and San Diego's first black licensed amateur radio operator. On the school's gymnastics team in 1940, he performed during halftime at Aztec basketball games. An engineering major, Coleman studied for three years at SDSU then six months at Cal Tech before working as a research engineer at MIT's famed Radiation Laboratory in Boston, Massachusetts during World War II. After the war, he got his bachelor's degree at UC-Berkeley, married and resettled in Valencia Park, and found employment at the Navy Electronics Laboratory in Point Loma where he labored for 32 years. Coleman helped to establish the Elementary Institute of Science and was a founding member of the Black Engineers Association of San Diego. Shortly before his death on June 17, 2008, he was named "Man of the Year" at Christ United Presbyterian Church.

Juanita R.L. Hayes

After attending San Diego State in 1944, Juanita Hayes left to complete her bachelor's degree at now defunct Leland College in Louisiana. She returned to San Diego and, as a library clerk, was one of the few blacks in the late 1940s hired by the city government in a non-custodial capacity. As a community college instructor, in 1973 she was named "Teacher of the Year," and in 1986 she was chosen a "Mother of the Year" by the *San Diego Union-Tribune*. She died February 5, 2011.

In terms of race relations, the 1950s offers some rather baffling and irreconcilable ironies. Take for instance the point that since the founding of the school in 1897 there had been considerably more students of Asians descent on campus (particularly Japanese and Filipino Americans and Asian foreign nationals) than black students. They even predated blacks on athletic teams. But as late as 1954 the people of Japan were referred to in headlines in the student newspapers as "Japs." In keeping with tradition, only a few photos of regular black students would appear in the student newspaper during the decade---all of the rest were affiliated with athletics. The newspaper's editors never made a serious attempt at airing black issues or to investigate race relations on campus or elsewhere. The decade also witnessed a resurgence of racial caricaturing on campus unmatched in any previous era. The usual culprits responsible for this were white social fraternity and sorority members.

From the perspective of the 21st century, one of the most disquieting things about the yearbooks up through the 1950s is the endless sea of photos of thousands of smiling Greeks, year after year with nary a dark-skinned person in the lot. It is here that one is confronted with the brutality of the racial caste system as it existed then. Among these thousands of photos only about 20 Asians and 20 Hispanics are evident. The white sororities were the most unrelenting in their devotion to racial purity as not even an Asian or Hispanic was allowed to discolor their ranks. Even more disturbing is the frequency of photos showing white Greeks in blackface performing some outrageous stunt thought to typify the African or African American experience, like a 1955 homecoming parade float rolling down a major boulevard with half-naked whites in blackface dressed as African headhunters, boiling a white hunter in a large pot. The float won the grand prize for the boys of Delta Sigma Phi. And it was not that the Greeks had cornered the market on such activity. A photo of frolicking white students at the Coronado Fine Arts Ball showed just

1950's

how artistic and creative they could be as they managed to caricature every darker-skinned race on the planet with their painted faces and outlandish costumes. For minority race students there was no escape from such unflattering depictions. To the chagrin of black Aztec football fans the half-time show featured a white male known as "Twinkletoes Thompson" in blackface wearing a tuxedo and white gloves who burst out in front of the marching band to sing "Mammy," conjuring up Al Jolson and the minstrel shows of the last century.

Not only was the social atmosphere for blacks in the 1950s for the most part uninviting, the employment situation for them on campus until the middle of the decade was a closed shop. For years even the lowest paying jobs on campus were denied to blacks. Group photos of secretaries, custodians, and groundskeeper revealed not a single black or person of color; and the first black professor who arrived 1956 did not hang around for long. In 1957 Jamaica-born Ira Lunan Ferguson (1904-1992), the author of several fiction and nonfiction books, arrived at SDSU for a job interview. Though with a Ph.D. from Columbia University he was told he was overqualified to teach here and that some white professors would feel uncomfortable in his presence.

Racial tensions never took a violent turn but an atmosphere of uneasiness about race pervaded Montezuma Mesa and this gave a superficial feel to racial interactions. In an interview with Harold Brown (Class of `59) a student leader and basketball great of the late 1950s, he recalled how blacks students congregated at Scripps Cottage to relieve the stress of academic life, to both commiserate and share their joys with other blacks. Poignantly, he also recalled that although he was a star player and widely known on campus, after basketball practice or a game he would not be invited to socialize off-court with his white teammates.³² Prominent black educator Ira Lunan Ferguson recalled in his autobiography that when interviewed for a faculty post here in 1957 he was told he was overqualified with his Ph.D. from Columbia University, a law degree and numerous publication, and that white faculty would have "problems of internal morale" if he was hired. Of course, he did not get the job. Nonetheless, there were some encouraging signs of progress. The recently formed Intercultural Club, the El Club Azteca founded to promote better relations with Latin Americans, and the International Relations Club each attracted a number of broad-minded students of various races and ethnicities. George Sunga, an Asian-American, was elected student body president in 1954. In May of 1952, the Westminister Club invited an interracial panel comprised of local Japanese-, Jewish-, African- (represented by civil rights activist and dentist Dr. Jack Kimbrough), and Mexican-American leaders "to better acquaint students with the position of minority groups in the San Diego area."³³ And that same month, after much discussion, the AS Council overwhelmingly approved a by-law crafted to "bar from the campus national organizations whose constitutions discriminate against race and religion,"³⁴ though ultimately this measure proved ineffectual.

Kappa Alpha Psi Sweetheart Ball (1958)

Julius Lester: One of the Best Kept Secrets

One of the best kept secrets about African American students at San Diego State is that one of them is the esteemed intellectual Julius Lester who has written two dozen books and retired as a professor at the University of Massachusetts at Amherst. Lester was an exchange student from Fisk University in the spring of 1959. He had a part-time job working in the library and in his 1976 autobiography, *All is Well*, he confessed to having a crush on one of the librarians.[35] In the book he also provided a glimpse of what it was like being a black student here at that time. In particular, he recalled how he became infuriated while watching white fraternity members in blackface singing spirituals at a student talent show (possibly the very same frat singers in blackface that appears in the 1959 yearbook). Lester started shouting and swearing at the frat singers and had to be restrained by some black students. Later, he wrote a letter to the editor of *The Aztec* which explained why he considered the performance to be insulting.[36] He said it got no response, but he may have been somewhat mistaken because after his lengthy, thought-provoking letter was published we can document only one other incidence of whites performing in blackface on campus. On a positive note, in his book Lester admitted that he was inspired by his literature class here and that it as at San Diego State that he began his apprenticeship as a writer.

Marlene Elizabeth Long: Paragon of Altruism

In the yearbooks of the late 1950s one black woman appears more frequently than any other in group photos of religious, pre-professional, and social service organizations. This is Marlene Long, then a chemistry major. Born in San Diego, Marlene graduated in 1959 and went on to obtain her M.D. degree at Howard University in 1963. She has worked as a Catholic Franciscan missionary/nun-doctor in several locations in Papau, New Guinea and Africa. Since 1996 she has worked with Surgical Specialist Outreach of the African Medical and Research Foundation (AMREF), Africa's largest indigenous health charity. Her specialties are leprosy and reconstructive surgery. As a plastic surgeon she has labored in war-torn areas across the continent treating mainly wounded civilians. She has also been a traveling consultant on cleft surgery in India and Pakistan Africa is where she had dreamed of working since childhood.[37]

1950'S PROFILES

Harold Brown (1959)

Harold Kenneth Brown: Star Student Who Returned Home

The first black to attain administrative rank at SDSU was Harold Brown (Class of '59) who during his student years here was president of Kappa Alpha Psi, the first black fraternity on campus chartered in 1951; a star basketball player who also lettered in baseball; and a member of Blue Key and the Wesley Foundation. As upper division student council representative, he fought to end discriminatory practices of fraternities and sororities. In the early 1960s Brown headed the local chapter of the Congress of Racial Equality (CORE) and was jailed repeatedly for demonstrating against discriminatory hiring at the Bank of America. He worked as a school teacher, Peace Corps officer, banker, and earned his MBA at Fordham University before returning to SDSU in 1971 as assistant to the vice president which entailed supervision of the new Afro-American Studies program and EOP. Currently retired, he was also Director of Community Economic Development (CED) in the College of Business Administration. Brown has been heavily involved in organizations that have assisted in the economic growth of Southeast San Diego. In 1997 he was elected president of the annual Holiday Bowl football game.

Harold Brown (1988)

Julius T. Campbell: Everybody's Role Model

Julius Campbell (Class of '56) represented the true spirit of an Aztec. In several yearbook photos as early as 1952 it was not apparent that Campbell, a sociology major, overcame more than racial prejudice to become one of the most admired students ever to attend this school. You could not tell by looking at his photo in a lineup of the seven brothers of Kappa Alpha Psi; and it could not be discerned in the photo of Campbell, the only black seated at a table casually smoking a pipe in a gathering of student leaders. Campbell became president of Kappa Alpha Psi, the first black fraternity chartered in 1951; and he was elected president of Associated Men Students, thereby becoming the first black to head a predominantly white campus group. It is not until we browse the 1956 yearbook which carried four separates shots of him, and see the one on page 208 that shows his full body in an upright position, do we began to realize what a struggle it must have been for this exceptional young man to beat the odds. Campbell was a paraplegic. In the photo--the only one revealing his disability—he stands with the aid of special crutches.

It was a tribute to him that his fellow students, black and white, recognized his abilities and courage and ignored his physical handicap, thereby allowing him to flourish as a student leader and to bring out the best in those who knew him. Twenty years after he enrolled at San Diego State, Campbell was working as Youth Division Director of the San Diego Department of Human Resources and serving on the Mayor's Council on Youth Opportunity. Born in 1933, he died in San Diego in 1985.

Leon L. Williams: City Councilman and County Supervisor

Considering the broad range of campus organizations he was involved in, and that he made it a habit to "dress for success" wearing his signature double-breasted coat and tie, it was obvious Leon Lawson Williams (Class of '50) had big plans for the future. After graduation there were administrative jobs with the San Diego Sheriff's Department, the Neighborhood Youth Corps, and the San Diego Urban League. Studying for a law degree from the University of San Diego further prepared him for the rigors of public office. Representing San Diego's 4th District, William served as city councilman from 1969 to 1982. In 1983, he was elected to the County Board of Supervisors and served as it first black chairman. His honors and awards, consultancies, and leadership in a host of important groups are two numerous to detail here. What many remember about Williams is his soft-spoken effectiveness and deep concern for the quality of life of all San Diegans. Named in his honor, the Leon Williams Scholarship Fund is administered by SDSU. In 2007 SDSU awarded him an honorary doctorate and a refurbished Room 430 in Love Library was dedicated in his honor. Witnessed by a crowd of more than 100 family members, acquaintances and dignitaries, on June 29, 2011 the SDSU Trolley Station was dedicated in his honor.

Beatrice Green Markey: First Black Faculty Member

Though her stay here was too brief it was nonetheless historic. In the fall of 1956, Beatrice Markey arrived as assistant professor of political science having just completed requirements for the doctorate in public administration at the University of Southern California with the help of a Hayes Foundation fellowship. Normally, *The Aztec* mentioned new faculty at the start of the academic year in a perfunctory manner with no fanfare whatsoever, but in Markey's case the editors took the unusual step of announcing her arrival with a headlined article and, just in case readers might miss the point that she was black because the article tactfully avoided specifying her race, they included a full-face photo of her worth more than a thousand words.[38] Unfortunately, by 1958 the 45-year-old professor was teaching at the University of Hawaii at Hilo, having had little impact on the school and soon forgotten. She died in Hilo in 1980.

Charles Bernard Bell, Jr.: Brilliant Mathmatician

Charles Bell had taught at his predominantly black alma mater, Xavier University in Louisiana, and Stanford University before landing here as this school's second black faculty member in 1958. Earning his doctorate in mathematics at Notre Dame University in 1953, he taught and did research at prestigious institutes and universities on four continents, among them the University of Paris, the University of Michigan, the University of Madrid, the Mathematical Institute in Amsterdam, the University of Gutenberg in Germany, the University of Vienna, Tulane University, the National Science Foundation, and the University of Washington. Bell published at least 39 mathematical papers in his areas of specialization: nonparametric statistics, stochastic processes and related application fields. He spent time in Nigeria developing curriculum for math teachers and worked with mathematicians in Calcutta, India. Bell, an affable but forceful individual who has long maintained an interest in African American history and culture, very much enjoyed working at San Diego State. Perhaps not surprising considering his globetrotting, his disjointed career at SDSU was from 1958 to 1966, then he returned to teach from 1981 until his retirement in 1992. He died in Los Angeles, October 26, 2010.

Earl Gilliam (1952)

Earl Ben Gilliam: Federal Judge

The totally unexpected discovery about his student days is that Earl B. Gilliam (Class of '53), the future U.S. District Court judge appointed by President Carter, is that he had a penchant for acting and, as seen in the 1952 yearbook, was cast in the drama department's production of the comedy "Dr. Knock." Finishing Hastings College of Law in 1957, he worked as a deputy district attorney in the San Diego District Attorney Office. He was a Municipal Court judge from 1963 to 1975; became San Diego's first African American Superior Court judge in 1975; and 1980 was elevated by President Jimmy Carter to the U.S. District Court, Southern District of California. Gilliam was also a law professor at Western State College of Law and he founded, organized, and served on the boards of quite a few local organizations and institutions. Wisely choosing to honor him while he was still alive, in 1982 the Association of Black Attorneys of San Diego County changed its name to the Earl B. Gilliam Bar Association in recognition of his unparalleled service to the legal profession and his community. Gilliam passed away in 2001.

George L. Stevens: City Councilman

An honorably discharged veteran in 1955, George Stevens (Class of '58) accompanied Dr. Martin Luther King Jr. on the historic Selma to Montgomery March in 1965. He led the San Diego chapter of CORE from 1967 to 1969, and was a board member of the NAACP. Stevens worked for several years at General Dynamics before making his first bid for a City Council seat in 1964, which was unsuccessful. Undeterred, he gained considerably more political experience as chief of staff for County Supervisor Jim Bates and later as Congressman Bates' special assistant. In 1991 he was elected to fill the Fourth District seat on the City Council. Forced to give up his Council seat in 2002 because of the term limit rule, he made a spirited, though losing effort to be elected to the California State Assembly. An associate minister at Mt. Erie Baptist Church, Stevens garnered over 100 citations and awards for his service to the citizens of San Diego. He died on October 11, 2006, seven months after the new $5.2 million George L. Stevens Senior Center in Martin Luther King Jr. Community Park was dedicated in his honor.

Robert Osby: San Diego Fire Chief

A sophomore at SDSU in 1959, Robert Osby was undecided about a career direction. While studying in Balboa Park he noticed a long line of young men applying to become firefighters and decided to join them. He worked himself through the ranks then left the city to become the fire chief in Inglewood, California and later San Jose. Osby was hired as fire chief of San Diego in 1992, supervising nearly 1,300 firemen and lifeguards. Osby retired from the SDFD in 2002 and became fire chief in Oceanside, California, resigning in 2005. He was chairman of the International Association of Metropolitan Fire Chiefs and a founder of the San Diego Chapter of the International Association of Black Professional Fire Fighters. In 2011 his son, Daryl, became the first black fire chief of Los Angeles County.

1950'S PROFILES

OTHER 1950'S NOTABLES

Richard David Ralston

Richard David Ralston Until his recent retirement Ralston (Ph.D., UCLA) was Professor of History and Director of the Department of Afro-American Studies at the University of Wisconsin at Madison. He was on the 1957 Debate Team.

Homer Floyd Broome

A member of Kappa Alpha Psi fraternity, Homer Broome (1931-2007) moved to Los Angeles and became the LAPD's first black patrol commanding officer in 1969. He rose to the rank of Commander. Known as a "bright and soft-spoken gentleman". The Southwest Police Station was named in his honor. Upon retirement he was appointed by President Carter to an administrative post in the U.S. Department of Justice. Bradley appointed him vice president of the Los Angeles Public Works Commission. Broome was the founding president of the Greater Los Angeles African American Chamber of Commerce was a board member of number of professional and community organizations. A bid for a city council seat in 1987, with the endorsement of Mayor Tom Bradley, was unsuccessful.

Duran Bell, Jr.

Duran Bell, Jr. Before transferring to UC Berkeley where he earned his Ph.D., Duran Bell (photo right), Emeritus Professor of Economics at UC Irvine, was a student at San Diego State from 1956 to 1957.

Tony Pinkins

For many years the all-time basketball scoring record was held by Tony Pinkins (Class of '58) who was also team captain. A victim of encephalitis in 1965, he was confined to a wheelchair but continued to work as an elementary school mathematics teacher in Indiana. On hand to honor him at a basketball game half-time ceremony in 1977 was Mayor Pete Wilson and other dignitaries.

Edward Sidney Fletcher

A standout player on the football team in the early 1950s, Ed Fletcher (Class of '53) worked for 36 years in the city's public schools. He retired as Assistant Superintendent of San Diego City Schools. Fletcher also worked as education director for the San Diego Urban League. In 2011 he was Alumni Diversity Award winner. He was president of the SDSU Veterans Alumni Chapter and is a member of the SDSU War Memorial Committee.

Evelyn S. Clark

Evelyn S. Clark (Class of '55) was the lovely Kappa Alpha Psi Sweetheart of 1955. She was awarded the doctorate in education in 1972 at the University of Southern California. Clark directed Multi-Services Family Center in Inglewood, California

Amos Johnson Jr.

A member of three campus religious groups, after graduation Amos Johnson (Class of '59) attended Maryland Baptist Seminary of the West in 1963. He was pastor of The New Creation Church in San Diego. He also sold insurance and became a certified financial planner.

August L. Castille

In 1975, August Castille (Class of '54) was principal of Penn Elementary School, and in 1988 he was principal of Fulton Elementary. A travel agent and owner of Easter's Park Travels for 32 years, he made an unsuccessful try for District E representative on the San Diego School Board in the year 2000.

Opalene Carter Mitchel

The Flo-Line Family Scholarship Fund was founded by Opalene Carter Mitchell (Class of '55) in Palo Alto, California. She authored the manual *A Stitch in Time: The Making of a Family Heirloom Quilt*, published by the Family Reunion Institute.

1940'S PROFILES

Hartzog & Kappa Queen

Ernest Eugene Hartzog

Varsity basketball player and multi-talented athlete Ernest Hartzog (Class of '55, '62) was the county's first black high school principal (Lincoln High in San Diego, 1970). He received his doctorate in social psychology in 1969 and was president of the 5000-member strong National Alliance of Black School Educators from 1979 to 1981. Hartzog later worked in the public school system in Portland, Oregon where he retired.

Robert L. Matthews

After completing his master's degree at Columbia University in 1955, Matthews wanted to move from teaching into public school administration so he took classes for certification at San Diego State. In an interview, he recalled that some professors were not encouraging but that one was very supportive and a good mentor.[39] Matthews went on to become a school principal and president of the Educational Cultural Complex in Southeast San Diego.

Thomas O. McJunkins

The third black faculty member was Thomas McJunkins (1919-1977), a graduate of Morehouse College and Atlanta University, as assistant professor of sociology from 1959 to 1965. He later became Associate Superintendent of the San Diego Unified School District in the 1970s.

Alyce L. Davis

The first black librarian at SDSU was Alyce Davis in 1959, a cataloger who received her M.A. degree from Columbia University. She died in Los Angeles in 1991.

William Glenn Moore

A grade school teacher from 1959 to 1966, Moore (Class of '57, '65) obtained his Ph.D. in education at the University of Oregon and began a second career working on various government related education projects in Oregon. By 1993 he was a research professor at Western Oregon State University.

Ferman David McPhatter

Ferman "Mac" McPhatter (Class of '52) was on the track team, played end on the 1950 championship football team, was football team co-captain in 1951, and was selected to play in two post-season bowl games. From 1953 to 1982 he was employed by the San Diego School District, earned his master's degree in administration at United States International University, and retired as Principal of Woodrow Wilson High School. In 1990, McPhatter Summit School was dedicated in his honor. Paralyzed in an automobile accident, he nonetheless participated in the National Veteran's Wheelchair Games for ten years. McPhatter died January 29, 2009.

Norvell Freeman Sr.

At age 14 Norvell Freeman Sr. was sent to Boys Town in Nebraska where he excelled in sports and graduated with honors. After a stint in the Navy he returned home, graduated from San Diego State (Class of '57) where he met his wife, then got a job as the first black employee of Jack-in-the-Box. He next worked as an employee of General Dynamics (featured in *Ebony* magazine in 1962, photo left) for 33 years and retired as Director of Industrial Relations in 1994. In retirement he was a San Diego Grand Juror. He died in 2009.

Barbara Louise Anderson

Born in San Diego, Barbara L. Anderson (Class of '54) became a certified librarian at age 20. Following service as young adult coordinator for San Diego's central (downtown) library and principal librarian in Riverside, in 1974 she became the first minority race person in California to head a county library system and the first African American head of the San Bernardino County Library which she directed until 1994.

Clarence E. Stanfield

A 1958 graduate, Clarence E. Stanfield (1930-1987) was an elementary school teacher, vice principal and principal in the San Diego Unified School District and a counselor and administrator in the San Diego Community College District. He also had leadership roles in several civic, education, and administrative organizations, including the Salvation Army, California Council of Adult Education, and the Association of San Diego Community College Administrators. A plaque honoring his memory is positioned near a tree on the campus of San Diego City College.

Grandison Madison Phelps Jr.

After pastoring churches in Massachusetts and Maryland, Rev. Grandison Phelps served as a Navy chaplain then located in San Diego where in 1955 he led the flock at St. Paul's United Methodist Church until 1992. He helped to launch the Southeast Interdenominational Ministry Alliance; the Gingerbread Day Care Centers which managed the area's first Head Start programs; and the federally assisted Bay Vista Methodist Heights Apartments. A graduate of Clark College and Gammon Theological Seminary, both in Atlanta, Georgia, he did graduate work at Howard University at Boston University, and last attended SDSU in the Fall of 1957. He also has the distinction of being the first black in San Diego to run for city-wide public office when in 1961 he ran for a seat on the school board, but lost. In 1963 he was narrowly defeated in a try for Fifth District councilman. He died August 17, 1997.

The
Civil
Rights
Movement was in
full swing by 1960 and
at the end of the decade the
country's military was bogged down in
a distant war in Asia, all of which gave rise
to widespread student protest and social upheaval
unlike any previous era in our history. San Diego State
would experience and reflect the kind of changes occurring in
society. The school's black students, faculty and staff would be at the
forefront of a revolution on campus.

As was the case with other large public institutions across the country, the school had to respond to the demand to allow more minority students access to higher education and it devised special plans and programs like EOP to help them cope. Many years later, Dr. Wayman Johnson (Class of `69) told a reporter for the *Los Angeles Times*: "All of a sudden, a lot of blacks were at a conservative, white campus. . . (EOP could) identify, understand and deal with an environment that (students) perceived as threatening, hostile unfriendly and, in some cases, even dangerous: the campus life at SDSU."[40]

For decades there had been only a tiny but brave corps of African American students here and the tendency was to keep a low profile, not complain or make waves, act like model students and hope that well-meaning whites would come to respect them. This mindset was evident when Julius Lester almost went berserk in 1959 upon seeing white fraternity members singing spirituals in blackface and was restrained by fellow black students who told him, "Don't act like a nigger."[41] This strategy was effective to some extent but it did not relieve their sense of social isolation and awkwardness in dealing with whites.

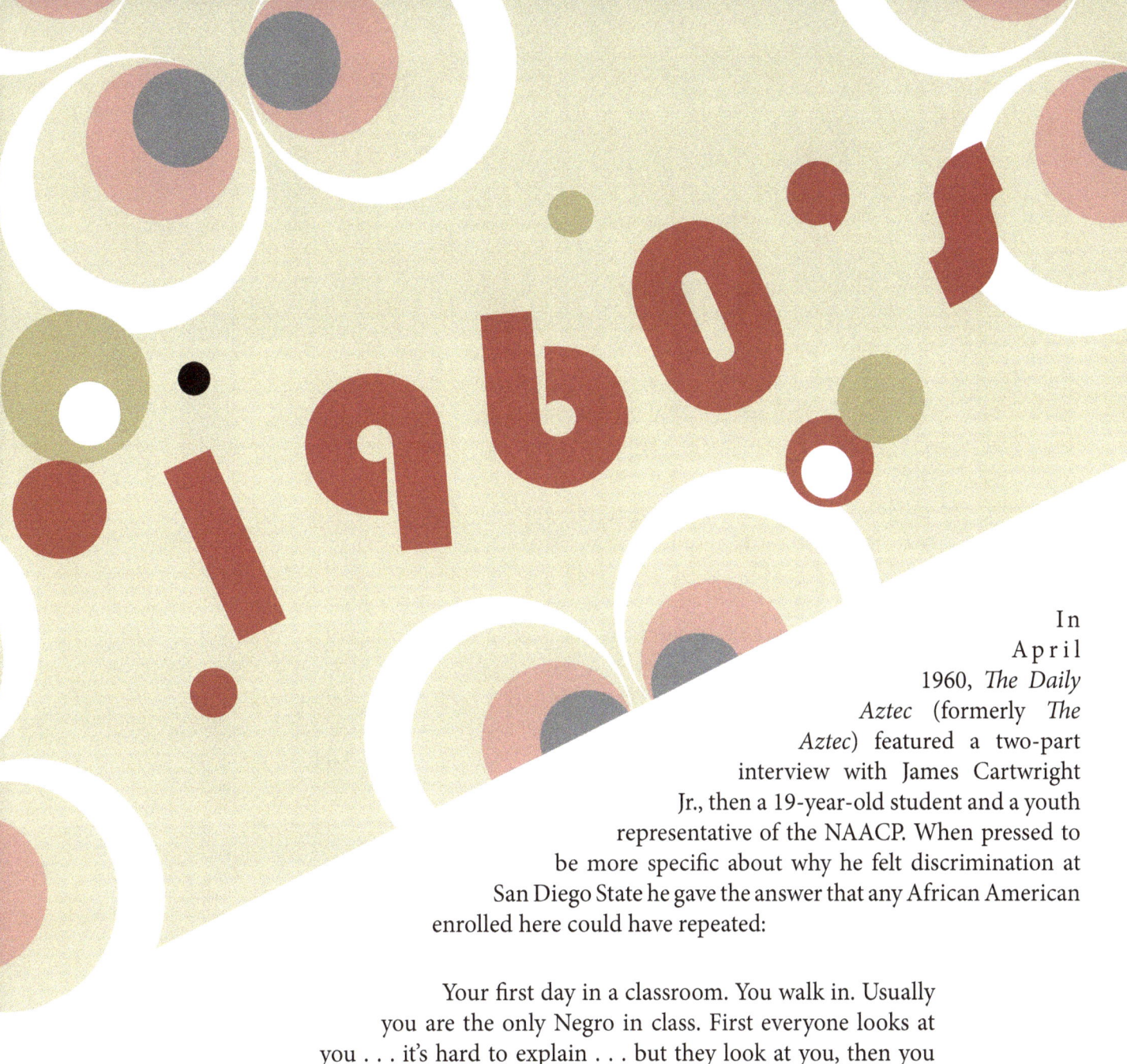

1960's

In April 1960, *The Daily Aztec* (formerly *The Aztec*) featured a two-part interview with James Cartwright Jr., then a 19-year-old student and a youth representative of the NAACP. When pressed to be more specific about why he felt discrimination at San Diego State he gave the answer that any African American enrolled here could have repeated:

Your first day in a classroom. You walk in. Usually you are the only Negro in class. First everyone looks at you . . . it's hard to explain . . . but they look at you, then you look away. It's almost as if they were embarrassed for you. Do you see what I mean? Then they ignore you . . . just like you weren't there, as if you were nobody.[42]

Odd as it may seem today, as late as 1966 San Diego State fielded an all-white men's varsity basketball team. However, by 1967 the Black Student Council was founded and black students felt bold enough to sponsor an annual celebration called "Black is Beautiful Week" during which proudly worn dashikis, humongous Afros, and Kinte cloth were the order of the day.

In his interview referred to above, James Cartwright Jr. was asked what he thought of the "radical tactics" used by the NAACP to protest discrimination. Cartwright replied: "We've got to be heard on things . . . and sometimes the only way we can be heard is to speak with force. If this is being radical, OK."[43] The Cartwright interview was prompted by the NAACP's picketing of stores in San Diego that had direct commercial ties to cities in the segregated South and the AS Council was being pressured to endorse a petition in support of the protest action. In June of 1963, the local chapter of the Congress of Racial Equality (CORE), headed by former student Harold K. Brown, was out in force at the intersection of El Cajon Blvd. and Fairmount with placards that read "Freedom Now" and "No Funds for Segregated Schools" as President John F. Kennedy's motorcade rushed to commencement ceremonies.

By the late 1960s there was good reason to be optimistic about the future of blacks on campus. The AS Council by-laws were changed in 1969 to reserve two seats for minority representation, one for a Mexican-American and one for an African American (John Coleman), with voting privileges on the council. The goal of having an Afro-American Studies major--an idea first suggested to university president Malcolm A. Love on the day of Martin Luther King Jr.'s assassination—was well on its way to becoming a reality.

The hardest nut to crack, the exclusionary policies of the social sororities and fraternities, was seriously confronted. Back in February 1945 an editorial in The Aztec titled "Intolerant Fraternities" bemoaned the practice of excluding Jews from college fraternities.[44] Nothing was said about the minorities of color as the idea of them integrating the fraternities was believed too improbable, perhaps unthinkable. A loophole in the measure passed by the AS Council in 1952 barring these groups from discriminating based on race exempted those chartered before 1949, thus allowing most of them to freely practice their old habit. The issue resurfaced in November 1962 when state attorney general Stanley Mosk came to SDSU and announced that sororities and fraternities who fail to delete discriminatory clauses in their constitutions should not expect to receive recognition on any tax-supported campus. President Love enforced a ruling that required all such groups to sign a non-discrimination pledge. All but four sororities refused to sign citing their constitutionally protected free right of association and claiming they feared being forced to accept someone (a minority race person) they did not want just to prove they did not discriminate. The upshot of all of this was that the fraternities and sororities no longer had the kind of power and influence on campus they were accustomed to.

Finally, in 1968 Reggie Richardson became the first black admitted into a predominantly white Greek social fraternity: Sigma Pi. Some other first time achievements by black students during the decade include Clyde Thomas (photo right) in 1960 as editor-in-chief of the *Aztec Engineer*, an impressive quarterly technical magazine that kept businesses informed about SDSU students in engineering, math, physics and chemistry; Ozy Reynolds, as a regular reporter for *The Daily Aztec* in 1964; Joan Knight (photo left) as head songleader for the football team in 1963; and Joyce Wilfong on the cheerleader squad in 1967.

There were a lot more black celebrities visiting the campus but none more distinguished or significant than Martin Luther King Jr. who dropped by on May 28, 1964. He spoke to a crowd that filled the Open Air Theater, telling them of the need for Congress to pass pending legislation that would protect the rights of blacks and improve their condition. He reasoned:

THE 1960'S

> You can't legislate integration but you can legislate desegregation. Morality can't be legislated, but laws can regulate behavior. Laws can't make you love me, but they can keep you from lynching me.[45]

In addition to Dr. King, other VIPs who spoke or performed on campus included Sammy Davis Jr., once billed as the world greatest entertainer, at Peterson Gym; tenor Roland Hayes who gave a recital, "Lieder of Many Countries"; comedian-activist Dick Gregory; jazz singer Ella Fitzgerald; civil rights activist James Farmer; syndicated columnist Carl Rowan; pop singer Dionne Warwick; psychologist Price Cobbs; militant Black Power advocate Stokely Carmichael; comedian Bill Cosby; and singer-actor Harry Belafonte.

E. Walter Miles: The Godfather of Black Faculty

The contributions of E. Walter "Wally" Miles to the good reputation of this university and, moreover, his importance to African American faculty and staff, cannot be overstated. As a graduate student at Indiana University, Miles spearheaded a campaign to desegregate public accommodations in Bloomington. He later mounted a successful boycott of white businesses in Hempstead, Texas and fought to improve off-campus housing at the University of North Carolina. A former U.S. Army officer who once rubbed shoulders with Colin Powell, Miles was the only black professor on campus when he arrived in the political science department in 1967.

More than a scholar who knew constitutional law and the judicial process (his specialties), Miles, a charming and gracious man, was a natural politician who was a master at getting things done behind and scenes. His knowledge about the inner workings of the university and his innumerable contacts here and outside SDSU meant that his sought after advice could save a person struggling to survive in a sometimes cutthroat environment, and he was always available to assist anyone. Miles worked tirelessly in the community and was widely know in his profession. He became chairman of the board of the San Diego Urban League; was chairman of the San Diego chapter of the American Civil Liberties Union (ACLU) and served on its national board; a trustee of the Center for Research and Development in Law Related Education; board member of Law in American Society Foundation; chairman of the Commission on the Status of Blacks in the American Political Science Association; associate editor of the *Western Political Science Quarterly*; and he was elected to the governing board of the American Political Science Association. One of his best moments was shown of local television in 1985 when he faced off on the topic of affirmative action with Clarence Pendleton, President Reagan's conservative black appointee who headed the U.S. Civil Rights Commission---a debate which Miles clearly won. By the end of the century Miles was chairman of the political science department and still as passionate as ever about protecting civil rights and undoing civil wrongs.

Cleavon Jake Little: Award Winning Actor

Despite his high school counselor's belief that he was not college material, Cleavon J. Little (Class of '65), who was raised in a Navy housing project in Linda Vista, refused to let this discourage him.[46] Today he is best known for his performance as the lead actor in (photo left) the 1974 comedy western movie "Blazing Saddles," directed by Mel Brooks and co-starring Gene Wilder. Little was a speech major who partially financed his college education through public readings of prose and poetry in the community. While at San Diego State he recorded a phonograph album of African American poetry with organ accompaniment titled "The Dreadful Hour" (1964) which was sold nationwide. Though generally thought of as a comedy actor, Little won a scholarship to study at the prestigious American Academy of Dramatic Arts in New York City and appeared on Broadway plays and in the New York Shakespeare

Festival production of "Hamlet." In 1970 he won the Tony Award for best actor in a Broadway musical comedy ("Purlie Victorious"). He starred in the movies "Vanishing Point" (1971), "Greased Lightning" (1976), "Cotton Comes to Harlem" (1970), and "Double Exposure" (1982). Little died in 1992.

Del Marie Neely Anderson: College President and Chancellor

Starting out as a high fashion model, Del Anderson (Class of '65, '67) veered into education, earning her A.B. and M.S.W degrees at SDSU. During her career as an Ebony Fashion Fair model she appeared on the cover of *Jet* magazine, December 7, 1961. Working in the state's junior colleges, she climbed the administrator's ladder to eventually become president of San Jose City College. From 1995 to 1998 she was Chancellor of the City Colleges of San Francisco, the nation's largest multi-campus community college (enrollment 95,000). Upon leaving CCSF a scholarship Fund bearing her name was established by friends and colleagues.

Roland McFarland: Major Media Executive

In the 1960s, Roland McFarland (Class of '64) was performing on stage at the Old Globe Theatre to sell-out crowds as the lead male actor in "A Raisin in the Sun" and "The Owl and the Pussycat." In addition to acting in many other plays around town, in Los Angeles, and at SDSU, he directed plays, performed in lecture-recitals, and received awards for his work. Formerly Vice President for Broadcast Standards and Practices for Fox Broadcasting Company, charged with overseeing the content of prime time and late night programming, today he occupies the same position at MyNetworkTV. McFarland, born in Haiti but mainly raised in San Diego, has been active in the Beverly Hills/Hollywood NAACP, a group that honored him with its President's Award.

Ambrose Jacobs: The Warrior-Scholar

He was just another athlete on the football team and that was pretty much all you could say about this young man in 1967. But Ambrose Jacobs went on to become a Lieutenant Colonel in the U.S. Army; attended the Army War College; was a troop commander in the elite Armored Calvary Regiment in Germany which later fought in Operation Desert Storm; earned a Ph.D. in political science at Stanford University; taught at West Point; was American Defense Attaché to the Republic of the Congo; and is currently a professor at Bennett College in South Carolina.

Napoleon A. Jones: Federal Judge

Napoleon A. Jones (Class of '62), like his predecessor and Kappa Alpha Psi fraternity brother, Earl B. Gilliam, also got his law degree at the University of San Diego and in a very similar fashion worked his way up to become a federal judge (U.S. District Court, Southern California District), appointed by President Bill Clinton in 1994. He died December 12, 2009 at age 69. In his obituary in the *San Diego Union* it was recalled: "One of Jones' most noteworthy decisions came in 2003 when he ruled that San Diego's lease with the Boy Scouts for land in Balboa Park was an unconstitutional violation of the separation of church and state."

Maulana Karenga: Militant Turned Academician

The long affiliation of Dr. Maulana Karenga with SDSU extends back to September 1967 when he spoke on campus at the invitation of the Black Student Council. At the time he was the leader of the militant nationalist group called US and he spoke surrounded by five intimidating bodyguards. His knowledge of Africa and African Americans deepened over the years and he acquired two Ph.D.s; taught courses for SDSU's Afro-American Studies department in the 1980s; became chairman of the Black Studies department at Cal State Long Beach; published scores of books and articles; and created the holiday celebration of Kwanzaa, for which he is widely known today.

OTHER 1960'S NOTABLES

David Lee Crippens

The first president of the Black Student Council (BSC), Crippens received his master's degree at SDSU in 1968 and worked in EOP. He moved to Pittsburgh to work as a newsperson and producer for WQED-TV. He later moved to Los Angeles and became Vice President of Educational Enterprises at KCET-TV overseeing educational programming for this award-winning public television station. Today Crippens serves a board chairman of Urban Possibilities, a Los Angeles area community rescue organization. He has been chairman on the Board of Directors of Unite-LA and president of the Los Angeles Workforce Investment Board Youth Council. In 2011 was appointed to the Los Angeles Universak Preschool (LAUP) Board of Directors by Supervisor Mark Ridley-Thomas." Crippens is also the owner of the consulting firm DLC & Associates. In the year 2000 his personal papers were stored at the University of Maryland.

Suswyn P. Mills

Returning to his native St. Kitts in the Caribbean after taking as many business courses as he could from 1962 to 1963, Mills became Finance Minister of the former British colony. He died March 14, 1989.

Clarence Stanley Crockett

Sometimes referred to as a free spirit and a firebrand, Dr. Crockett, who received his terminal degree from the Municipal University of Amsterdam, was a lecturer in the English department from 1964 to 1967. His outspoken stance against the school's employment record in regards to non-academic employees and the discriminatory and "undemocratic" history fraternities and sororities was reported in *The Daily Aztec*. He once told a student reporter: "San Diego has a reputation for being an unfriendly city for Negroes. . . I would be glad to see less (Red Cross) blood giving and more tutoring in low income schools (by SDSU) students."[47] Dissatisfied with the progress of race relations in this country, Crockett left San Diego and stayed in Mexico for a while before returning to the city in 1970 to join the staff of the Western Behavioral Sciences Institute in La Jolla.

Vernon Sukumu

Former head of the Black Federation and director of the Welfare Rights Organization who founded the city's first homeless and women's shelters, longtime social activist Vernon Sukumu (photo left) was president of the Black Student Council in 1968. Born Vernon Fontenette Jr. in New Iberia, Louisiana, aside from his community activism, until recently he co-owned of the Aswan Restaurant in La Mesa.

Thomas E. Logans

Thomas E. Logans President of Oceotl, a predominantly white men's service fraternity, and Kappa Alpha Psi social fraternity, Thomas Logans (Class of '65) was also vice president of Blue Key and Kappa Delta Pi. Listed in *Who's Who In American Colleges and Universities*, he was on the varsity wrestling and track teams too. His younger brothers, twins Elmer and Eddie, were on the tract team in the mid-1960s.

Wilhelmina Elaine Perry

A social work professor from 1968 to 1978, Dr. Wilhelmina Perry was among the first group of five first African Americans to attend the University of Texas at Austin. In 1998 she interviewed her partner, Puerto Rican activist and former SDSU professor Antonia Pantoja, for the *Harvard Business Review*. With Pantojo she co-founded a school to train local community activists called the Graduate School for for Urban Resources and Social Policy, Inc. in San Diego; and the Latino Educational Media Center in 2001.

Ernest Fredrick Anderson

Ernest Frederick Anderson Graduating with a master's degree from San Diego State in 1967, E. Frederick Anderson completed his doctorate at USC and returned to teach at SDSU in 1973. Before leaving in 1981, he rose to become Associate Dean of the College of Health and Human Services. Anderson is now Professor of Social Work at Cal State Los Angeles. He is married to another distinguished SDSU alumnus, Del M. Neely Anderson, mentioned above.

Haven Moses

Haven Moses Most Valuable Player on the 1967 Aztec football team, Moses was the first Aztec to be picked Division I All-American. He was a first round draft choice of the Buffalo Bills and later played for the Denver Broncos. He now works as director of community outreach for the Archdiocese of Denver. His name is on the "Ring of Fame" at Invesco Field.

Shirley Mae Gissendanner

Running for the U.S. Congress in 1982, Gissendanner (Class of '68) defeated her illustrious opponent, football's Heisman Trophy winner Mike Garrett, in the Republican primary contest but lost to the Democrat challenger in November. In 1973, she was a lecturer in Afro-American Studies. She died at age 70 in 2013.

Eric R. Moaney

With an M.F.A. from Syracuse University and with considerable experience working in advertising and graphic art firms, Prof. Moaney began teaching at SDSU in 1968 and picked up a master's degree in counseling here while doing so (Class of `75). He retired in 1998.

Elbert Alexander Colum

Elbert Alexander Colum Dr. Elbert "Al" Colum (Class of '62) was appointed principal of Gompers Junior High School in San Diego in 1969 and later was assistant superintendent of the Berkeley Unified School District and lecturer/supervisor at Notre Dame de Namur University in Belmont, California. Born in Kansas, he was in the Navy during the Korean War. In retirement he served on the board of trustees at Fort Scott Community College. He died in 2008.

R. Eunice Aaron

Prof. Eunice Aaron (Class of '62) earned her law degree and taught in the Black Studies department at San Francisco State University from 1980 until she retired in 2005. She has served in the statewide Academic Senate of the California State University and has been very active as a union official representing lecturers on her campus.

Lillian Kennedy Beam

The library on the campus Nairobi, Kenya campus of Alliant International University (formerly United States International University) is named in honor of Dr. Beam (Class of '68) who was also director of the Education Cultural Complex in San Diego in the early 1980s. She has been vice chancellor of U.S.I.U., director of East Africa Coalition for International Trade in Dar es Salaam, Tanzania; Kenya coordinator for Teachers for Africa; and founder and administrator of World Econoculture. She died at age 84 in 2008.

Taylor A. McKenzie

McKenzie got is B.A. (1969) and M.A. (1971) at SDSU and then finished his Ph.D. at the University of Southern California. He is a professor in the speech department at Grossmont College and is the senior minister of the Church of Christ at 61st and Division Streets in Southeast San Diego.

Leon Henry Osborne

While chairman of the art department at Fresno City College, Osborne (Class of '67, photo left)) was honored at SDSU in 1975 as one of its distinguished alumni. Born in San Diego, he was in the Army during World War II. A member of the SDSU Alumni Association and Phi Kappa Phi Honor Society, he died in 2007.

Gwendolyn Patrick-Buie

A library assistant who was hired in 1967, Gwen Patrick-Buie was elected vice president of the California State Employees Association (CSEA) in 1996 and co-chairperson of the Study Commission on Black Affairs (SCOBA) in the early 1990s when it confronted President Day on his administration's affirmation action record. She handled numerous grievance complaints by staff personnel and received the CSEA's Community Service Award in the year 2000. She retired in 2007.

Wayman H. L. Johnson

A 1969 graduate, Dr. Johnson taught computer and information science for 15 years at San Diego Mesa College before becoming an administrator there. He retired from the college as Dean of Learning Resources and Instructional Support Services. The founding of a black SDSU alumni organization in 1991 grew out of Johnson's idea for a reunion among SDSU students who participated in the first black Equal Opportunity Program which ran from 1969 to 1972.[48]

Efiong O. Andem

After getting his master's degree in microbiology in 1968, Dr. Andem finished his medical degree at Howard University. He returned to his native Nigeria twice but has spent most of his professional career working as a doctor for the U.S. Air Force. He was chief medical officer at Holmes Correctional Institution and is currently in private practice in Bonifay, Florida. A devout Christian, he also serves as the directing physician at Faith Health Clinic in nearby Marianna.

Donald Frederick Shy

The owner of Papa Shy's Gourmet Barbecue Restaurant in Oceanside, Don Shy, a world-class hurdler, was also a running back for the Aztecs and played pro ball beginning in 1967 with the Pittsburgh Steelers, then the Chicago Bears, New Orleans Saints, and finally the St. Louis Cardinals in 1973.

Mercedes H. Ritchey

Receiving her master's degree at San Diego State in 1963, Ritchey was principal of Lincoln High from 1971 to 1974. She died May 2, 2007.

Raymond Quintin Collymore

Raymond Quintin Collymore Collymore (Class of '65) was awarded a Kellogg Fellowship and received his doctorate in higher education from the University of Colorado. He was local stage actor and former Marine, and director of the College Learning Center at Johnson County Community College in Kansas. He died in 1978.

Raymond L. Dorrough

A dentist practicing in Pittsburg, California, Dr. Dorrough (Class of `69, `73) graduated with honors from dental school in 1977 and then acquired a Ph.D. in theology (again with honors) from the International Theological Seminary. When he is not extracting teeth at Raymond L. Dorrough Family Dentistry he is preaching the gospel at Love Christian Fellowship World Outreach Church. He is the author of the book *Latter Reign: An Omnipotent God and His Omnipresent Kingdom* (Shippensburg, PA: Treasure House, 1993).

Maurice Jackson

Dr. Jackson was Assistant Professor of Sociology from 1962 to 1965. He left to teach sociology at UC Riverside where he also chaired Ethnic Studies. He died in 1987.

Kern Carson

Kern Carson The hero of the celebrated 1962 Aztec versus Fresno State football game, Carson played for the Baltimore Colts. He coordinated community services for UC San Diego and was manager of the Ebony Inn in San Diego. In March 2002, Carson operated a transitional living center for ex-convicts in Riverside County where he was found murdered in his home. His attacker was caught and convicted.[49]

Katye Anderson

Katye Anderson For 22 years Katye Anderson (Class of '64) was a professor at San Diego Mesa College where she founded and headed the school's Black Studies department and was twice named Teacher of the Year. She died September 21, 1992 at age 69.

George W. Pearson

21-year-old George W. Pearson Jr., who had been senior class president at Lincoln High School, while a junior at SDSU was drafted into military service. He was killed in action while rushing to aide his comrades in October 1969 in Tay Nihn, Vietnam, and remains the sole African American listed on the SDSU War Memorial.

Stephen J. Andrews

A member of the SDSU chapter of Kappa Alpha Psi fraternity, Stephen Joseph Andrews (Class of '65) worked for 25 years for Union Bank of California. He was promoted to branch manager of the bank's location at the intersection of Federal and Euclid. Prior to his death at age 67 on July 19, 2007 he had served on the boards of Neighborhood House Association, Southeast Rotary, and the San Diego County Retirement Board.

Laurie Lee Center

Secretary of the Black Student Council, social science major Laurie L. Center (Class of '68) became president of the California Math Council-Southern Section. Her distinguished career in elementary education ended when she died in 1996 but her good work is honored via the council's annual Laurie Center Elementary Teaching Award given to a K-6 teacher who "has demonstrated outstanding work with students of color," and the Laurie Center Scholarship given annually to three exceptional teachers of color.

Tendayi Kumbula

Tendayi Kumbula Retired Ball State University journalism professor Dr. Tendayi Kumbulu (Class of '68) was awarded his doctorate in education at the University of Southern California in 1976. He was been a fellow in the American Press Institute, the American Society of Newspaper Editors, and the Poynter Institute of Media Studies. He was a member of the National Alliance of Black School Educators Minorities and the Media, National Association of Black Journalists, and the Society of Professional Journalists, among others.

Fannie Lois Jeffries Payne

Fannie J. Payne (1915-2008) arrived with her husband in San Diego in 1942 with a degree from Talladega College in Alabama. In the post-war years they both became pioneering public school teachers. In 1964 she got her master's degree from SDSU.

Payne retired from teaching in 1979 and devoted more time to such organizations as Delta Sigma Theta Sorority, Links Inc, and Talladega Alumni Association, Altrusa Club of San Diego, Delta Gamma International Society, and received several honors for her exceptional service, including a Woman of Dedication recognition by the Salvation Army.

Rudolph Allister Johnson Jr.

Born in El Centro, Rudolph "Rudy" A. Johnson Jr. (1944-2009) graduated from SDSU in 1962 then enlisted in the U.S. Air Force. He returned to SDSU and obtained a master's degree in social work. After a stint at Cal State-San Bernardino as EOP director he worked as director of youth services for the Neighborhood House Association and eventually became its Deputy Director. In 1982 he was selected President of the San Diego Urban League. In 2001 he retired as Director of Youth Services for the City of San Diego.

Claudette Johnson

The first African American graduate of SDSU to appear on the cover of a major magazine was Claudette Johnson whose attractive face graced *Jet* magazine's October 3, 1963 issue. Johnson worked her way through school with a job in the library. Later, she was employed as a clerk San Diego Police Department, a technical librarian for General Dynamics, and as a secretary for San Diego Congressman Lionel Van Deerlin when she switched gears and became a fashion model. Not only did she appear on *Jet*'s cover, she also was in three other photos in the magazine's feature story on her career. As a former Ebony Fashion Fair Model she appeared again in *Jet* in 1982 celebrating the fair's 25th anniversary in New York City.

Otis L. Jones

After finishing his undergraduate work at SDSU, Vallejo, California attorney Otis L. Jones got his law degree at the University of San Diego then worked for the Legal Aid, was a Deputy District Attorney, became and real estate broker and a business law professor. A former president of the California Association of Black Lawyers and the Association of Black Attorneys of San Diego County, he has been the legal counsel for many community groups, churches, and organization.

1960'S PROFILES

Andre Henderson

SDSU alumnus Andre Henderson (1945-2010) launched many businesses during his life. He once owned as many as thirteen Taco Bells. Departing the business world in the late 1980s, he went into the ministry eventually serving as pastor of San Diego's Highland Park Church from whence he sent missionaries abroad and instituted "Linking America to Africa" (later renamed the Andre Henderson NonProfit in his honor) with the goal of "teaching business and leadership in African Communities."

Arthur Joseph Graham

Playwright Arthur J. Graham (Class of '67), a native of Jamaica, was granted the Ph.D. in English literature at UC-San Diego in 1980. He is noted mainly for his plays about black life penned in the late 1960s and early 1970s, among them *The Last Shine*, *The Nationals: A Black Happening in Three Acts*, and *Daddy Was a Welfare Check*. At SDSU, he co-founded the Afrikan Student Union with Judge Napoleon Jones (see above) in 1968. In 2009 Graham was listed as a faculty member of the Amen-Ra Theological Seminary and he has also taught as an adjunct professor at Arizona State University.

Hollis Smith

Hollis Smith was a graduate student here in 1963. Having spent 18 years in the aerospace industry he became CEO of the Green Power Foundation which helped to develop second generation businesses. In the early 1980s he was the founding president of the Southern California Minority Business Development Council and for 25 years watched it grow and become the state's main advocate for minority business development. Retired in 2000, he lives in Indio, California and remains active in community groups.

Robert C. Moss Jr.

At present an adjunct sports faculty member at the University at Arkansas-Pine Bluff, Bob Moss (Class of '61), or Bob "Hubba Jubba" Moss as he likes to be called, was on the Aztec football and baseball teams in the late 1950s and early1960s (his father was the first black to play on the Aztec basketball team). He worked as a teacher and counselor in the San Diego Unified School District from 1965 to 1971 and was on the faculty of the physical education department of UC-San Diego from 1971 until he retired in 1992. A published author on sports topics, Bob also enjoyed his work as a motivational speaker and consultant.

Thomas E. Logans

A defensive player on San Diego High School's football team and a hurdler, broad jumper, and wrestler for the Aztecs, Tom Logans was one of the three Logan brothers (along with Eddie and Jerry) who were on the SDSU track together in the 1965. After graduation Tom left for Houston, Texas where he worked in government, sales, construction, business operations and management, and became Vice President at Access Data Supply, Inc.

Clifford T. Johnson Jr.

Clifford T. Johnson Jr. An electrical engineering graduate (Class of '69) who later obtained an MBA at the University of Phoenix, Clifford Johnson worked for McDonald Douglas, General Dynamics, Boeing, and for twelve years was a systems engineering manager at Northrop Grumman. A member of Omega Psi Phi, he has served of the executive board of the Scripps Ranch YMCA.

Houston Robert Ridge

Houston Robert Ridge, Jr. Picked in the thirteenth round of the AFL draft in 1966, Aztec defensive lineman Houston Ridge (1944-2015) played for four seasons with the San Diego Chargers. However, he is probably best remember for having filed a class action lawsuit against his pro football league for injuries suffered as a player. He and others believed disabilities that ended their careers were the result of steroids and amphetamines given to players. Ridge eventually reached a settlement with the Chargers for $250,000. In his post-football career he was a financial advisor, the father of one child and stepfather of several. Born in Madera California, he died in San Diego and was buried in Mt. Hope Cemetery.

With the backdrop of the still raging Vietnam Conflict, Kent State shootings, Senate Watergate hearings, exposed illegal CIA operations, a hostage crisis in Iran, California's passage of Proposition 13, and still catching its breath caused by the swift changes of the 1960s, the campus of San Diego State, now officially called a university, would continue to experience pressures related to it steady growth and the challenges of an even more ethnically diverse campus. Since 1969 there had been an interdisciplinary major in Afro-American Studies that took advantage of courses offered to students by several departments, but by 1972 these students had a home in the newly established Department of Afro-American Studies. Comments made a year earlier by the program's coordinator, Frances S. Foster, who along with Lonnie Briscoe and Cedric Bryant wrote the proposal establishing the new discipline that was accepted by the University Senate, reflected the times and the original intent of those who pushed to institute a discipline centered around the "black experience" in America and aimed specifically at black students. Foster was quoted in *The Daily Aztec* as saying:

> "We can't, of course legally exclude non-Blacks from the courses we offer. But because our resources limit the number of classes that maybe offered, Blacks will have first priority. We are dealing with self-image of Blacks, not just information… We will determine who is to be admitted by means of an informal interview. We want students to understand that these courses will not be G.P.A. inflators. Rigorous standards will be observed. These classes will not be a place for rapping, ideological confrontations or easy As."[50]

1970's

Two situations may best exemplify the complexity of a rapidly changing social climate on campus which sparked tensions but found peaceful resolution. One was the creation of the Black Pep Squad in 1970, financed by the Black Student Council (BSC), which competed behind the football field sidelines with the long established SDSU Cheerleaders squad. The idea of the Black Pep Squad was to introduce a style of entertainment black fans and others could better appreciate. A compromise was soon reached and the two squads integrated.

The other situation, more serious, had to do with the long history of complaints black students had about *The Daily Aztec*'s coverage (or lack thereof) of issues "Black is Beautiful Week" pertaining to black folk. Things came to a head in November 1971 when a performance by singer Roberta Flack received a lackluster review in the newspaper which, as some charged, had failed to promote the event and in typical fashion, the newspaper's critics charged, found a minor point to criticize and blow out of proportion. Two BSC members confronted the white editor and one of his reporters in the newspaper's office. A photo of their tense face-to-face standoff was captured for the newspaper.[51] The BSC members demanded better coverage of black events and an apology. They also threatened to come back and shut down the operation and tried to get the AS Council to freeze the newspaper's funding. This got everyone's attention. Black students demanded an investigation, which they got. Eventually, the AS Council censured the newspaper, the editor resigned, and the position of Minority Editor was created to insure that the interests of African Americans and Hispanics would be taken into account.

"Black is Beautiful Week"

67

THE BLACK IN CRIMSON AND BLACK

For a while a special page in the newspaper headlined "The Third World" publicized minority events and lasted until it was agreed that such events were being integrated into other campus news. Still, black students felt that token gestures were not enough so they took the initiative and published several newspapers and magazines on their own, something that has occurred periodically until now.

On May 13, 1970, 31 students were arrested at SDSU because of a sit-in demonstration held here in sympathy with black students killed and wounded by Mississippi state police at Jackson State University. On May 24, 1972 a bomb place in the hallway ceiling on third floor of Tarastec Hall where black students had been racially harassed exploded and injured Lawrence Jackson. A week prior racist graffiti had been painted on a sidewalk and on cars owned by black students. Two other noteworthy occurrences in the decade deserve mention. One is the rise and decline of the Black Communication Center which occupied a house on Hardy Avenue and was headed by Corrine M. Conway, a former president of the BSC. The center served as a haven for black students and a place for cultural enrichment and getting practical advice, but it lacked sustained funding. Outside of the BSC, black students were finding greater acceptance in campus organizations. Undoubtedly, the best example was the election of Cal Robinson as the first African American president of Associated Students. Other black student body presidents would follow and they are listed below:

Corinne Conway

1. Cal Robinson 1973-1974
2. Daniel Walker 1988-1989
3. Journard Collins 1991-1992
4. Dwayne Crenshaw 1992-1993
5. Ron Williams 2001-2002
6. Priscilla Ocen 2002-2003
7. Chris Manigault 2005-2006

Cal Robinson

Daniel Walker

Journard Collins

Celebrities visiting SDSU in the 1970s include civil rights activist Julian Bond; former Black Panther leader Eldridge Cleaver; singer Ray Charles; poet Gwendolyn Brooks; Black Muslim spokesman Minister Louis Farrakhan; and writer Alex Haley.

Shirley Nash Weber: The Mover and Shaker

For most of its existence Dr. Shirley Weber was chairperson of the Department of Africana Studies (formerly Afro-American Studies). Retired in 2010, for decades she had been among the most influential and distinguished professors at SDSU. An advisor to black faculty and staff and a willing role model and mentor for students, the recipient of outstanding faculty awards, she earned her academic degrees at UCLA, arriving on campus in 1972. Twice elected to the San Diego School Board on which she served as president, Weber also ran for the City Council and the County Board of Supervisors. Her leadership in organizations is quite extensive and much appreciated as evinced by the numerous awards and citations she has received. She is a dynamic public speaker who is often requested to give the keynote address for important events across the nation. A was President of the National Council for Black Studies, the most prominent organization promoting Black Studies in higher education, and Executive Director of San Diego's Association of African American Educators. Running as a Democrat in the 79th District, on November 6, 2012, she won a seat in the California State Assembly, thus becoming the first African American elected to represent a district in San Diego County in the state legislature in Sacramento. She trounced her Republican opponent, a La Mesa businesswoman, by 21,460 votes.

She was reelected to the California State Assembly in 2014 and shortly thereafter was appointed to chair the Assembly Budget Committee. Eleven of her bills were signed into law and six of her resolutions were passed during her first term. She was reelected again in 2016.

Carl Weathers: Hollywood Actor

Best known for his role as the flamboyant boxer Apollo Creed in the movie "Rocky" (1976) starring Sylvester Stallone, Carl Weathers (Class of '70), a theater major, played football at SDSU and was a linebacker for the Oakland Raiders. He had the lead role in "Fortune Dane" (1986), "Action Jackson" (1988), "Hurricane Smith" (1990), and the TV movie "Dangerous Passion" (1995). Weathers also was the lead actor in the TV series "Street Justice." In 1982, he was master of ceremonies at the annual alumni banquet and was surprised when Deputy Mayor Lucille Killea proclaimed May 19 "Carl Weathers Day" in San Diego. In recent years he has appeared in television sitcoms.

1970'S PROFILES

Roland Wentworth Boniface Bullen: Diplomat

Born into a well-to-do family in the Caribbean, Roland Bullen (Class of '71) earned his master's degree in public administration at U.S.I.U. in 1973 and entered the Foreign Service in 1977. He worked at various locations around the world. By 2000 he was the most senior diplomat in the Eastern Caribbean. Working out of the American Embassy in Barbados, Bullen was Charge d'Affaires for Grenada, St. Kitts and Antigua, Dominica, St. Lucia, St. Vincent and the Grenadines. In 2002, he was reassigned to Washington to be Deputy Executive Director, Bureau of Western Hemisphere Affairs (WHA) at the U.S. State Department. In 2003 he became U.S. Ambassador to Guyana, and in 2006 was deputy chief of mission to the U.S. Embassy in the Dominican Republic.

Arthur Leon Ellis: The Good Samaritan

Arriving in 1978 in the social work department with a doctorate from Columbia University, Arthur L. Ellis said that the turning point in his life was meeting Martin Luther King Jr. during the Montgomery Bus Boycott. He initiated two local self-help organizations designed to uplift and inspire black youth; served as chairman of the city's police review board; was a member of the California State Task Force on Mental Health and Juvenile Delinquency; was on the San Diego Human Relations Commission, and served on SDSU's Academic Senate. In 1995, he was an Outstanding Faculty awardee chosen by the SDSU Alumni Association. Soft-spoken, highly articulate, pleasant and charming, he was a natural for radio and television interviews. Ellis never lowered himself to pettiness or attacks on others but instead devoted his life to bringing people together. He died of lung cancer in 1996.

Herman Edwards: NFL Head Coach

As of this writing, there are only five black head football coaches in the National Football League, and one of them is Herman Edwards (Class of '71) who graduated from SDSU with a degree in criminal justice while playing cornerback for the Aztecs. He spent most of his pro years as a player with the Philadelphia Eagles and was an assistant coach under Tony Dungy (another NFL black coach) at Tampa Bay before he was picked to lead the New York Jets in January 2001. In 2006 he was made head coach of the Kansas City Chiefs, a job he kept until 2009. In 2005 he published the motivational book *You Play to Win the Game* (McGraw-Hill). He has also worked as a football analyst for ESPN.

Frances Smith Foster: Eminent Scholar

Hired in 1971 as an assistant professor of Afro-American Studies, Foster S. Smith became full professor of English and Assistant Dean of Student Affairs for the College of Arts and Letters before leaving to teach at UC San Diego in 1988. She also headed the campus chapter of Phi Beta Kappa. Foster is now at Emory University where she is Charles Howard Candler Professor of English and Women's Studies. An authority on American slave narratives and African American and women's literature, she has published six books, among them the *Oxford Companion to African American Literature* (Oxford University Press, 1997) and *Witnessing Slavery: The Development of Ante-Bellum Slave Narratives* (Greenwood Press, 1979). In 2010 she received the Modern Language Association's Jay B. Hubbell Medal, the first black female to be honored for lifetime achievement in literary studies.

Fahari Jeffers: Union Leader and Board Chairperson

Working for three years with Cesar Chavez who taught her and other blacks organizing skills, and further inspired by her mother who was a maid, Fahari Jeffers (Class of '75), co-founded and became secretary-treasurer and general counsel of the United Domestic Workers of America/AFSCME (UDW), the nation's first union for domestic workers representing 12,000 members in California. An attorney, Fahari became chair of the board of the San Diego Convention Center in 2000. She also is the mother to several adopted children.

Anthony Keith Gwynn: Baseball Superstar

Probably no alumnus of SDSU is more wide known than Tony Gwynn who enrolled here in 1977. A star athlete on two sports teams, he was drafted in 1981 by both the San Diego Clippers to play professional basketball and the San Diego Padres to play baseball. Of course, he chose to play baseball and proved to be one of the game's best pure hitters ever. In 2007 he was inducted into the Baseball Hall of Fame and special exhibits relating to his career were featured in the University Library. His record of accomplishments is too lengthy to adequately summarize here. Gwynn's unusually clean image as a family man and volunteer contributor to community projects further endeared him to San Diegans. In 1997, Tony Gwynn Stadium was christened at SDSU in his honor. Upon Gwynn's retirement in 2001, he was named to take over as head coach of the Aztec baseball team. Though not generally known, not only did Gwynn play on the Aztec basketball team but he "remains the only athlete in WAC history to be honored as an all-conference performer in two sports." Gwynn died on June 16, 2014.

David "Smokey" Gaines: Basketball Coach of the Year

A former Harlem Globetrotter, Gaines introduced his unique style of basketball honed as head coach at the University of Detroit. The first of two black head basketball coaches at SDSU (Tony Fuller was the other from 1992 to 1994), Gaines produced five winning teams at SDSU between 1979 and 1987; took the team to the NIT Tournament; was named Western Athletic Conference (WAC) Coach of the Year in 1985 after a 23-7 season; and was assistant athletic director from 1987 to 1988. Gaines has owned several businesses including five restaurants (the latest is Smokey's II on Campo Road in Spring Valley) and has contributed to various community groups. In 2005 he was named athletic director and head basketball coach at LeMoyne-Owen College in Tennessee. He is currently Athletic Director for the Memphis (Tennessee) City Schools.

OTHER 1970'S NOTABLES

Sharon Beatrice Grant-Henry

Sharon Beatrice Grant-Henry In 1986, returning alumnus Dr. Sharon Grant-Henry, who earned a master's degrees from SDSU and doctorate from Princeton University, began teaching counseling and school psychology at SDSU in the College of Education. In 1964, at age 14, she was the youngest member of CORE marching alongside her parent protesting racial discrimination in San Diego. She took medical retirement in 1998, and died February 3, 2004 at age 54.

Fred Norfleet

Fred Norfleet Former Channel 10 KGTV "Spectrum" talk show host Fred Norfleet (Class of '73), owner of Norfleet Video Productions, was elected to the SDSU Alumni Association Board of Directors. He has done outstanding volunteer work in the San Diego community. In 2010 he was award an alumni Monty.

Michael G. Johnson

Graduating with honors in 1974, Johnson became principal of Granger Junior High School in National City. In 1994, he was honored as SDSU Distinguished Alumnus.

Willie Buchanon

Willie Buchanon An All-American cornerback on the Aztec football team during the 1970-1971 season, Willie Buchanon (Class of '73), who was born in Oceanside, played for the Green Bay Packers and the San Diego Chargers and was twice selected to play in the Pro Bowl. A former president of the Aztec Athletic Foundation, today Buchanon is a real estate broker in Oceanside.

1970'S PROFILES

Eugene E. Wigginton

Eugene Wigginton (Class of '76) achieved the rank of Major in the Rhode Island National Guard. A veteran of the Vietnam War, he worked for 32 years in state government. He died in 2007 and was buried in the Rhode Island Veterans Memorial Cemetery.

Arnie Paul Robinson Jr.

The second Aztec to win an Olympic gold medal, Robinson (photo left), a native of San Diego who attended Morse High School, took the gold in the long jump in the 1976 Olympics in Montreal. All totaled, he captured two Olympic medals (bronze in 1972 in Munich, gold in Montreal), won the 1971 Pan American Games championship, and seven national AAU title in his events. Robinson coaches track at San Diego Mesa College. He earned his B.A. and M.A. at SDSU. In 2003, he was picked by the USA Track and Field Association to help coach the U.S. team at the World Outdoor Championships in Paris.

Felicia D. Washington

Ms. Washington (Class of '78) became director of sales for Pro-Line Corp. in Dallas, Texas.

Alton L. Reynolds

In 1984, Alton Reynolds (Class of '77) was business manager of local television Channel 69. He was a U.S. Air Force cryptographer during the Vietnam War and taught accounting at San Diego Mesa College. He died in 1986 at age 43.

Terrie Griffith

Once a faculty member at the Caribbean College of the Bible, Dr. Griffith (Class of '77) is executive pastor of the Greater Malabar Christian Centre (Trinidad and Tobago).

Emory Joel Tolbert

Emory Joel Tolbert Following a wrenching, well- publicized tenure battle at UC San Diego, Dr. Emory J. Tolbert taught briefly in the Afro-Americans Studies department, 1983 to 1984. He left SDSU for Howard University where he became full professor and chairman of the history department. Tolbert has been the principal author, co-author and editor of six books, among them *The UNIA and Black Los Angeles: Ideology and Community in the American Garvey Movement* (CAAS/ University of California, 1980).

Carrol Walter Waymon

In the early 1970s, psychologist Dr. Carrol Waymon taught Afro-American Studies here. Leaving SDSU, he taught for the next 25 years at San Diego Mesa College, where he retired. Known around town as a social activist, gadfly, and organization leader, he authored the book *On Being Black in San Diego: Anytown U.S.A.* in (WW Publications, 1994).

Daryl E. Rasuli

Daryl E. Rasuli Returning from military service in Vietnam, Rasuli (born Floyd) attended SDSU in the late 1970s. In New York state he was editor of the *Buffalo Challenger*, a black community newspaper; worked for the Urban Development Corp in New York City; became manager of communications for the Niagara Transportation Authority and president of the board of the Buffalo Federation of Neighborhood Centers. He was profiled in the 1989 edition of *Who's Who in the East*. When not dealing with issues related to urban transportation and community development, he writes poetry.

Marian Y. Foster

Named City Heights branch manager for Union Bank of California in 2002, Foster attended SDSU in the 1970s.

Carolyn Jacobs

Carolyn Jacobs A 1971 graduate with a master's degree in social work, Dr. Jacobs took her Ph.D. at Brandeis University in 1978. She is Dean of the School of Social Work and Elizabeth Marting Treuhaft Professor at Smith College in Massachusetts. She has trained as a spiritual director at the Shalem Institute for Spiritual Formation and has a spiritual direction practice. Her latest publication is "Exploring Religion and Spirituality in Clinical Practice, in *Smith College Studies in Social Work*, 80(2-3).

Esther J. Langston

Dr. Langston received her M.S.W. at SDSU in 1970 and a Ph.D. at the University of Texas. She is Professor Emeritus of Social Work at the University of Nevada at Las Vegas.

Nkem Nwankwo

In 1976, Dr. Nwankwo was a lecturer in the English department. His novels, like *Danda* (Collins, 1964) and *My Mercedes is Bigger Than Yours* (Harper & Row, 1975), have been compared to the writings of Chinua Achebe, the famed Nigerian novelist. Nwankwo was a professor of English at Tennessee State University when he died in 2001 at age 60.

John A. Berteaux

Berteaux (Class of '73) graduated "with distinction" in philosophy and eventually got his master's and doctorate at UC San Diego. In 2000 he moved from lecturer to a tenure track position in the philosophy department at SDSU but in 2004 left to teach at Cal State Monterey Bay where he became Associate Professor of Philosophy.

William H. Payne

The second black teacher hired by the San Diego Board of Education, Payne started his 25-year career in public schools at Pacific Beach Junior High in 1945 (white parents there fought mightily to have him removed) and retired at San Diego High. He was a lecturer and admissions director in SDSU's College of Education where he worked from 1970 to 1976. Payne died in 1986.

Robert Fikes, Jr.

Hired in 1977, Fikes published quite a few journal, magazine, and newspaper articles and several monographs mainly pertaining to African American history and literature and the achievements of the descendants of Africa in Europe and Latin America. His co-authored 1981 article, "Black Pioneers of San Diego, 1850 to 1900," for which he wrote most of the text, was made into a booklet and widely distributed by the San Diego Historical Society. In 1993, the California Court of Appeals ruled in favor of Fikes and a Latino colleague who had filed an excessive workload grievance, supported by their union, which reaffirmed the faculty status and rights of librarians. Fikes was editor of the newsletter of the California Black Faculty and Staff Association from 1979 to 2001. He also wrote two online books concerning SDSU's black and military alumni. Honors include Africana Studies Department Unsung Hero Award (2004), SDSU Monty for Outstanding Faculty (2007), Earl B. Gilliam Bar Association Award for Community Service (2009), and NAACP W.E.B. Du Bois Scholarship Award (2011). He retired in 2012.

Doris F. Givens

Doris F. Givens In 2000 Dr. Givens (Class of '77, '78) was named President of Spokane Community College, and in 2003 she was chosen interim president of West Los Angeles College and in 2006 was selected Provost of El Camino College's Compton Center. She had previously worked at San Diego City College teaching Black Studies and as a dean at Palomar College. In August 2011 she began her duties as the first black president of Kansas City Kansas Community College (enrollment 3,000+).

Curtis Morning Jr.

Mr. Moring attended SDSU from 1978 to 1980. He became president and CEO of Curtis Moring Insurance Agency Inc. and has been very active in professional and community groups.

Cedric Gael Bryant

Cedric Gael Bryant A lecturer who specialized in African American literature, Dr. Cedric Bryant, who worked at SDSU from 1973 to 1983, completed his Ph.D. at UC San Diego and became chairman and Lee Family Professor of English at Colby College. He was selected Maine Professor of the Year in 1996 by the Carnegie Foundation for the Advancement of Teaching.

Eddie Spencer Meadows

Eddie Spencer Meadows Although his home department was music (since 1972), Dr. Eddie Meadows also taught courses in the Africana Studies department. He published a number of articles and monographs largely dealing with jazz and the music of African Americans. He went to Ghana on a Fulbright fellowship and has lectured at UCLA, UC Berkeley, and Michigan State University. He retired in 2006.

Vinnie Romell Foster-Owens

Chosen the first black Miss San Diego at the annual pageant in 1972, Romell Foster was among the 10 finalists in the Miss California contest that year. She married a pro football player in 1975 in a wedding ceremony attended by local celebrities including Mayor Pete Wilson and Padre outfielder Dave Winfield. At SDSU she was a theatre arts and television production major and she studied film directing at the American Film Institute. Today she owns Jowharah Films. Two films she produced, "Native New Yorker" and "Pins and Needles," were official selections of the 2008 Cannes Film Festival. Aside from some award-winning films she has produced and written hundreds of hours of television programming. She has been honored with an NAACP Image Award and a Black Filmmakers Hall of Fame Award.

Richard Arnold Hill

Before he started as head track coach in 1972, Dr. Richard "Dick" Hill had trained some of the nation's best talent like Olympic gold medalists Willie Davenport and Bob Hayes. He led the SDSU track team to its first WAC championship in 1980. Hill left SDSU in 1981 to become athletic director at Southern University in Louisiana, then athletic director at the Massachusetts Institute of Technology (MIT). He retired as Dean of Student Life at MIT in 2003.

Jesse Owens Smith

A University of Chicago-trained political scientist, Dr. Smith taught in the Afro-American Studies department in the late 1970s. He became president of the California Black Faculty and Staff Association and by 1984 was a member of the Afro-Ethnic Studies faculty at Cal State Fullerton where he became a full professor and chairman of the department. He retired in 2005.

Phillip Timothy Gay

With a Ph.D. from Harvard University, Dr. Gay arrived at SDSU in 1976. He became chairman of the sociology department and in 2001 McGraw-Hill published his book, Modern South Africa. Aside from his academic work, Gay starred in movies, acted in local plays, and penned a television screenplay. In 2003 he penned the novel *Academic Affairs: Love and Murder in Academia* (Authorhouse) He retired in 2007.

Clyde W. Oden

Clyde W. Oden After attending San Diego State from 1962 to 1964, Dr. Oden got his O.D. (Doctor of Optometry) degree from UC Berkeley. He was president and CEO of UHP Healthcare Inc. in Los Angeles; chairman of the board of directors of WATTSHealth Charities; sat on the board of directors of the American Association of Health Plans; and served on the advisory council of the Director of Centers of Disease Control Prevention. Currently, he is a member of the Board of Visitors of the Graziadio School of Business and Management, Pepperdine University, and Chairman Emeritus of Medicaid Health Plans of America. An ordained minister, he is also senior pastor at Bryant Temple A.M.E. Church in Los Angeles.

Walter S. Hawkins

Long-time community activist Walter Hawkins (M.W.S., Class of '72) is director of Research and Policy Analysis at Cal State San Bernardino. He has served as a board member of the Rialto Unified School District and has worked with a coalition of African American leaders affiliated with the Westside Action Group in San Bernardino. Running as a Democrat, in 2004 he made an unsuccessful bid for the California State Assembly, District 62.

The Blevins Family

Possibly the record for the largest number of siblings from one family to attend SDSU is held by the Blevins Family. The seven children of David and Marie Blevins who attended SDSU mainly in the 1970s were: David Jr., Mary, Robert, Clifton, Patricia, Robert, Donald, and Ronald. Ronald and Donald were president and vice president of the Black Student Council in 1970.

1970'S PROFILES

Harold Surratt

Harold Surratt A telecommunications major in 1978, Surratt has acted in plays and Hollywood movies, including "The Pelican Brief" (1993) and "The Devil's Advocate" (1997), and the Hallmark Hall of Fame 1995 production of "The Piano Lesson." TV credits include "ER," "The Practice," "Fringe", and "Orange is the New Black.

Annjennette Sophie McFarlin

Annjennette Sophie McFarlin During the 1970s, Dr. McFarlin was director of Black Special Services and a lecturer in the Afro-American Studies Department. She became chairperson of the Speech department at Grossmont College (retired in 2002) and is known in the area as a community activist and professional storyteller. She taught at several colleges and universities across the nations. McFarlin founded the Black Storytellers of San Diego, Inc. and, as director of an intern program that found positions for black faculty in community colleges, she was recognized for her effectiveness by the State Chancellor's office. Born in 1935, she died November 26, 2013.

DeEtta M. West

The sister of actor Cleavon Little (Class of '65), DeEtta West, a music major, left SDSU in 1970 to work in the entertainment industry as not only as an actress, singer, talk show host, and voice-over artist, but also as an office employee at such firms as Tri-Star Pictures, KNXT-TV, KACE Radio, Elektra Asylum Records, Warner Brothers, etc. By 2002 she was executive assistant to Jamie Kellner, chairman and CEO of Turner Broadcasting Inc. in Atlanta, Georgia. Married to Rev. James A. West, DeEtta is also a licensed minister and works for the Gospel Music Channel.

Kasimu-Richard Harley

Mr. Harley began work in EOP in 1981 as a recruiter and was employed by the Student Resource Center when he left in 1988 to work in the community. He was dedicated and had a penchant for communicating with young people. Harley was the co-founder of the African American History Society at Bell Junior High and was a pupil advocate working with the city's Student Advocacy Program. He has worked as a marriage and family therapist.

Marvalene Hughes

A professor and counselor from 1972 to 1977, from 1977 to 1986 Dr. Hughes was Director of Counseling and Career Placement at SDSU. She left SDSU for administrative posts at the University of Toledo and the University of Minnesota. In 1994 Hughes was President of Cal State Stanislaus, and in 2005 was named the first female president of historically black Dillard University, resigning in 2011.

James Princeton Adams, Jr.

In 1976, Dr. Adams was a lecturer in social work at SDSU. He later earned his doctorate at the University of Minnesota and became Dean of the School of Social Work at the University of Alabama, then was named to occupy the same position at the University of Kentucky in 2008.

Ellen D. Nash

With her painted portrait enshrined on a wall of a Lincoln Park store with other community leaders, Ellen Nash (Class of '79), who works as a manager in SDSU's Human Resources office, received recognition for her work in Southeast San Diego among those struggling on the margins of society. Nash has also been active in SDSU's black alumni organization and in professional and community groups.

E Percil Stanford

A professor of gerontology in the College of Health and Human Services, and for many years director of the Center on Aging, Dr. Stanford, here since 1973, published widely and is an authority on black and minority senior citizens. On October 19, 2004 he gave the inaugural presentation of the E. Percil Stanford Lecture and Seminar Series, named in his honor. In retirement be became western regional director of the American Association of Retired Persons (AARP). In 2011 he founded and headed Folding Voice LLC, a gerontology consultancy, and was president of KIND Corporation, an organization that finds housing for low-income elderly in San Diego.

1970'S PROFILES

Hozell C. Francis

The pastor of Emmanuel Baptist Church in Inglewood, California, Rev. Francis (Class of '77) authored the book *Church Planting in the African-American Context* (Zondervan, 1999).

Rulette Villarante Armstead

The first woman to attain the rank of Captain on the San Diego police force, Armstead (Class of '74, '88) advanced to Assistant Chief of Police in 1992. In 1989 she was chosen Woman Police Officer of the Year by the International Association of Women Police. She has lectured in the criminal justice program at SDSU. In 2004 she was inducted into the San Diego Women's Hall of Fame with the designation "Activist." To the delight of students who consistently praised her, in retirement she taught criminal justice from 2002 to 2010 at SDSU.

Olita Elizabeth Dargan

Olita Elizabeth Dargan Harris A professor of social work since 1979, Dr. Harris was also Associate Dean of the College of Health and Human Services. She retired in 2013.

James Nwannukwu Kerri

James Nwannukwu Kerri A native of Nigeria, Dr. James Kerri (1942-2011) was an Afro-American Studies professor from 1977 to 1983, and he was made chairman of his department. He is presently a board trustee of ProjectChange International Inc., a group in Wilmington, Delaware that strives to protect Africans from preventable diseases.

Isaac Curtis

Drafted by the Cincinnati Bengals in 1973, wide receiver Isaac Curtis spent his entire NFL career there (1973 t0 1984). He holds the team's career receiving record of 7,101 yards. He is a sales executive for a hotel management firm near Cincinnati, Ohio.

Robert Lee Wood

Mr. Wood (Class of '73) used his accounting degree to become a financial consultant and opened a real estate brokerage firm 40 miles southwest of Atlanta, Georgia. A Democrat, in 2001 he became chairman of the Coweta County Commission (Coweta County population 90,000). In 2004, upon ending 12 years in public service, a community center was named in his honor.

Shirley Wade Thomas

Shirley W. Thomas   Charles W. Thomas

Shirley Wade Thomas A professor in the Afro-American Studies department from 1972 until her death in 1988, Dr. Thomas was a popular figure in the city's black community and a widely recognized expert in the field of black child development. Her husband, Dr. Charles W. Thomas, a prominent psychology professor at UC San Diego who was slain in 1990, occasionally taught and spoke at SDSU.

Danny Lyon Scarborough

Scarborough (center) and his troupe

A highly energetic artist, Dr. Scarborough founded the SDSU Black Repertory Total Theatrical Experience shortly after his arrival in the Afro-American Studies department in1977. His innovative Scarborough (center) and his troupe interpretive dance troupe comprised of students won an Emmy in 1979. An avid collector of African American art and artifacts, Scarborough succumbed to AIDS in 1989.

Abdur-Rasheed Muhammad

Born Myron Maxwell, Army Lt. Col. Abdur Muhammed was a graduate student in anthropology in the late 1970s when he turned from Christianity to Islam and became the first Muslim chaplain (Imam) in the U.S. military. Service in Iraq 2004 to 2005. Currently, he is associated with the Islamic Society of North America.

Woodrow Jones, Jr.

A political scientist, the administrative ambitions of Dr. Woodrow Jones Jr. (at SDSU from 1974 to 1991) were not encouraged here, so he packed his bags and left for Texas A&M University where he soon became Dean of the College of Liberal Arts. He died on November 22, 2005.

Patricia Delores W. Oyeshiku Worthy

A Peace Corps worker in Brazil and a recruiter before she got her master's in education, Dr. Oyeshiku (Class of '71) became an exceptional school teacher. In 1981, while at Morse High, she was named California State Teacher of the Year, and was a National Teacher of the Year finalist. She is retired.

Raymond Crump Howard

Employed here from 1974 to 1989, Dr. Howard was a well-liked professor of counselor education who retired to his native Montana where he died in a hospice in 2013.

Louis Cleveland Green

Employed at SDSU since 1976, Dr. Green was Professor of Economics who specialized in international trade and finance. He retired in 2003.

Cheryl Alyece Williams Fisher

Leaving in 2006 as director of SDSU's Office of Diversity and Equity, Cheryl Fisher (Class of '71), who has a law degree from the University of San Diego, served on the boards of the San Diego Metropolitan Credit Union, Girls Scouts, San Diego Opera, and chaired the western region community advisory board of Union Bank of California and the board of San Diego's Neighborhood House Association. In 2014 she was Senior Procurement Specialist for San Diego Contracting Opportunities Center. Her book is titled *To Mrs. O With Love* (2013) a collection of essay by her former students.

Vernon Oakes

Chairman of the Afro-American Studies department in 1973, Vern Oakes moved to Washington, D.C. where he worked as an administrator in the MBA program at Howard University and later started his property management company, Oakes Management Inc.

Robert Val Guthrie

Dr. Robert Guthrie moved to San Diego in 1960 and taught at San Diego Mesa College where he was the only black instructor. He was award the Ph.D. in psychology at the United States International University (now Alliant International University) in 1970; taught at the University of Pittsburgh; worked in the National Institute of Education in Washington, DC; and in 1976 returned to San Diego to work at the Naval Personnel and Development Center. Best known as author of the classic *Even the Rats Were White: Historical Views in Psychology* (Harper, 1976) which heralded the achievements of black psychologists and showed how white psychologists have viewed blacks, Guthrie periodically lectured in Afro-American Studies at SDSU in the 1970s and 1980s. He died of brain cancer in 2005.

Claudie Minor

Aztec Hall of Fame tackle Claudie Minor became a star player for the Denver Broncos. After his gridiron career he owned an operated Premier Enterprises (oil exploration and natural gas marketing), Premco holdings, and Premier Energy Supply. He has also been involved in inner-city real estate development projects in Denver.

Norman E. Chambers

Professor of Africana Studies at SDSU after nearly three decades of service in the department, Norm Chambers was a popular teacher and student organization adviser who in 2001 was selected an Outstanding Black Educator of San Diego County by Phi Delta Kappan. A clinical psychologist, Chambers obtained his master's degree from SDSU and Ph.D. from United States International University. He was director of the Carl Rogers Institute of Psychotherapy and co-director of the African Cultural Literacy Center and co-director of the African Cultural Literacy Center He also headed the Human Behavior and Urban Development Center which counseled students. He retired in 2001.

Florence Gilkesson

The first tenure track faculty member in the Afro-American Studies Department, Prof. Florence Gilkesson arrived in 1972, however she left to travel to Africa and attend graduate school at UCLA. Today she runs a family-owned mortuary in Indiana.

Georgette Katye Bartley

A 1975 graduate, Georgetta K. Bailey (she preferred being called "Katye") got her Ph.D. at U.S.I.U. in human development and enjoyed a long career at SPAWAR where she worked as a configuration manager. Quite active in the community affairs, she died in January 2003.

John M. Gissendanner

Another early recruit of the Afro-American Studies Department was John M. Gissendanner. Like Frances Foster and Florence Gilkesson, he had been a graduate student at UCSD. Gissendanner taught English at Towson University in Maryland and taught as exchange faculty in Japan and the United Kingdom. He died in retirement in 2008. A memorial lecture series at Towson was named in his honor.

Charles Dee Rucker

Though he was a police officer for 17 years who gained notoriety as a composite artist, and taught criminal justice at Southwestern College for two decades, Charles Rucker (Class of '75) is best known for his exquisite paintings of African Americans and life in Africa, the West Indies, and Mexico. His work--mainly done in acrylic, oil, and watercolor-- has been exhibited in galleries around the world, including the Brockman Gallery in Los Angeles. Prints have been sold in the Michaels arts and crafts store chain. The Charles Rucker Gallery is located on Adams Avenue in Normal Heights. Rucker died October 29, 2003.

Tayo Peter Olafioye

A celebrated Nigerian author of 18 books of fiction, poetry, and criticism, Prof. Olafioye taught in the English department from 1974 to 1976. He subsequently worked at a number of colleges and universities in Southern California, and he has returned to visit Nigeria and the University of Llorin where he once lectured. Born in 1948, he died in 2012.

Joseph Maurice Samuels

A professor of education, Dr. Joe Samuels, here from 1972 to 1982, was the university's first affirmative action officer. Prior to arriving at SDSU he was a past president of the Springfield, Massachusetts NAACP, a minister in the Massachusetts Church of God in Christ, a visiting professor of education at Appalachian State Teachers College, a teacher in the Upward Bound program at the University of Massachusetts, and an administrator and professor at Norfolk State College in Virginia.

George Hutchinson

A former U.S. Navy captain, Dr. Hutchinson was a professor of recreation/leisure studies in 1973. He later held administrative posts and worked in student outreach until he retired in 1994. After leaving SDSU he became a county government outreach worker assisting the homeless and others.

La Verne E. Ragster

Born in St. Thomas, U.S. Virgin Islands, LaVerne E. Ragster obtained her M.S. in biology at SDSU in 1975 then a Ph.D. in biology at UC-San Diego in 1980. She returned home to the University of the Virgin Islands where she taught marine biology, chaired the Division of Science and Mathematics and increasingly became involved in university administration and professional and non-governmental activities. In 2002 she was named President of the University of the Virgin Islands leading its 2,600 students and faculty, the fourth person and the first woman to hold this post. In 2010 she returned to the U.S. to received UC-San Diego's Professional Achievement Award.

Michele Jacques

Early Since 2004 Dr. Michele J. Early (Ph.D., Emory University) has been Assistant professor of Theology and Ethics at the Samuel DeWitt Proctor School of Theology at Virginia Union University where she also is director of the theology school's D.Min Program. Born in Los Angeles, she was a 1978 graduate of SDSU with a major in public administration and a minor in Afro-American Studies.

1970'S PROFILES

Robert Andrew "Bobby" Meacham

Currently the third base coach for the Houston Astros, a job he previously had with the Florida Marlins, Bobby Meacham attended San Diego State from 1979 to 1981 and played Aztec baseball with Tony Gwynn and Padres manager Buddy Black. His pro career included six seasons as a shortstop for the New York Yankees where he led the American League in sacrifice hits in 1984 and 1985; minor league manager and support posts for several major and minor league teams; and the 2007 season as San Diego Padres first base coach. He later worked as a base coach for the New York Yankees (2008) and the Houston Astros (2010-2012), then managed two minor league teams.

Walter Kudumu

An SDSU Extension student in the early 1970s, Walter Kudumu had moved from Louisiana to San Diego in 1948 when he was age nine. He became of the city's most prominent activists for childhood education and community improvement. One of the first individuals in the region to celebrate Kwanzaa (he had been a member of the local chapter of US), he served on numerous boards and committees and founded and co-founded several groups—among them the Center For Parent Involvement in Education and Black Men United--and was nationally recognized for his voluntary work. Mr. Kudumu died of cancer on April 8, 2008.

Willie Edward Hopkins

Willie Edward Hopkins After obtaining his bachelor's degree in 1977 and MBA in 1979 at SDSU, Willie E. Hopkins was granted the Ph.D. in business policy/strategic management at the University of Colorado in 1984. He taught at the University of Colorado, Colorado State University, University of Northern Colorado, University of Akron, and California State University at Hayward (now East Bay) before arriving at the University of Maryland Eastern Shore in 2004 as Dean of the School of Business and Technology. In 2005 he traveled to the opposite coast where he was Dean of the College of Business at California State University at Chico. Hopkins has authored numerous articles and has published two books: *Aligning Organizational Subcultures for Competitive Advantage* (Basic Book, 2005) and *Ethical Dimensions of Diversity* (Sage Publishers, 1997).

Nina Tucker

In 2008 Nina Tucker retired as Assistant Professor of Social Work at Oral Roberts University in Tulsa, Oklahoma. She had earned both her bachelor's degree in 1973 and master's degrees in 1989 in social work at SDSU.

Steven Clete Bradford

Thrice elected Gardena, California city councilman, Steven C. Bradford became the council's first African American member in 1997. After attending SDSU he graduated from Cal State- Dominguez Hills then worked as an IBM marketing representative, a recycling coordinator for the Los Angeles Conservation Corps, and solid waste director for the City Compton. An award-winning member of Phi Beta Sigma, when not attending to council business Bradford worked as a regional manager of public affairs for Southern California Edison.

Steven L. Coons

Steve Coons (Class of '73), the son of pioneering SDSU gymnast and coach Orlando Coons Sr., was a jovial and popular Black Studies and political science instructor at San Diego Miramar College. As a member of the college's Diversity Committee he was instrumental in organizing multicultural events and as a supporter of human rights he helped launch model United Nations and Amnesty International on campus. Coons, a grandfather and a role model to students, lost his battle against prostate cancer on December 1, 2008.

Vallera Johnson

In 2009 the Women's Law Division of the National Bar Association gave its Jurist of the Year Award to Administrative Law Judge Vallera Johnson (Class of '71, marketing). In 2008 she was honored with the following awards: the Outstanding Justice Award from the SDSU chapter of pre-law fraternity Phi Alpha Delta; the Mentor Award for Diversity Leadership from the California Western School of Law; the Diversity Award from the South Asian Bar Association of San Diego; and the Thurgood Marshall Legal Professional of the Year from the Earl B. Gilliam Bar Association. A Lawyers Club member, she has been the organizer of the Women of Color in the Law luncheons. Her law degree was earned at Howard University.

1970'S PROFILES

Harold V. Rucker

Presiding Administrative Law Judge Harold V. Rucker (M.A., political science, 1971) is on the California Unemployment Appeals Board. A former Deputy District Attorney and later a partner in private practice, he has taught business law and administrative law for paralegals at Cuyamaca College as an adjunct professor, and he currently teaches business law, organizational leadership, political science and history at Southern States University. From 1994 to 1995 he was President of the Administrative Law Judges Association (ALJA) and from 1981 to 1985 he was Judge Pro Tem of the Superior Court.

Mary E. Cox

For nearly three decades Mary E. Cox (Class of '70) represented juveniles in Virginia courts. In 1988 she was state coordinator for the Jesse Jackson Presidential Campaign. She has served as a board member of Richard Community High School, the Richmond Chamber of Commerce, and the Richmond United Way. In 1990 she was an independent candidate for mayor of Washington, D.C., and in 1998 she ran for a seat on the Washington, D.C. Board of Education. A 1978 University of San Diego Law School graduate, she worked in the College Park, Maryland firm of Blair & Lee.

Ralph Edward "Mitch" Mitchell

As government and public affairs manager for the San Diego Division of Hewlett-Packard Company, Mitch Mitchell directs the company's efforts in philanthropy, media relations, community and political relations. After acquiring both his bachelor's in television and film and master's in educational technology, he worked for television stations in Arizona and San Diego (KFMB) before joining Hewlett-Packard.

Patricia A. Harvard-Hinchberger

From 2002 to 2003 Dr. Patricia A. Harvard-Hinchberger, a registered nurse who received her master's degree in educational technology from SDSU (Class of '77), worked as a nursing educator and research faculty member at King Faisal Specialist Hospital in Saudi Arabia. From 2005 to 2007 she was President of Sigma Theta Tau nursing honor society, Xi Theta Chapter. Today she is Assistant Professor of Nursing at Cal State-Dominguez Hill. Most recently she taught at Cal State-Los Angeles. In 2012 she was inducted into the National Black Nurses Association Institute of Excellence.

James and Patricia Gordy

In 1979 one of the most lavish and star-studded Bel Air wedding ceremonies was that of San Diego State University graduates Desiree D'Laura Thomas (Class of '78) and Terry James Gordy (Class of '79), son of the Motown Records founder Berry Gordy. Attendees included Marvin Gaye, Diana Ross, Lionel Richie, Jim Brown, Lynn Swann, Smokey Robinson, and Alex Haley. A few years later Desiree got her law degree at Southwestern University School of Law and became a prominent member of the region's black business community. She remains in Los Angles practicing---what else?--- entertainment law. Terry is a branch manager of Sage Financial Advisors

Charles Kahalifa King

The founder and CEO of Harmonious Solutions, staffed by six multiethnic professionals offering counseling services ranging from conflict resolution to bereavement, is Charles K. King, an SDSU alumnus. For eighteen years he worked in sales and marketing before switching to psychotherapy. He has taught as an adjunct professor at SDSU and the San Diego Community College District. His local business has served such clients as the Superior Court, the U.S. Post Office, and private companies.

Ollie Matson

Groundbreaking sports star Ollie Genoa Matson II (1930-2011) was the second black coach at SDSU. From 1971 to 1975 he coached running backs on the football team. As a young man Ollie won Olympic bronze in the 400 meter and silver in the 4x400 meter relay in the 1952 Summer Olympics held in Helsinki, Finland. As a football player at the University of San Francisco he was a Heisman Trophy contender and was equally impressive as a pro football star on four teams. He was inducted into the Pro Football Hall of Fame in 1972.

Kathleen E. Harmon

For twenty years Kathleen Harmon was a nurse at Mercy Hospital. She also worked as a social worker/counselor at the House of Hope, a boy's group home. Then, in 1978, she earned double master's degrees at SDSU. A former vice chairperson of the County Democratic Central Committee (she was a California delegate to two national Democratic Conventions) and a long-time member of the Black Political Action Committee (BAPAC), she was active in election campaigns and once ran for the State Assembly.

Linda Gooden

The Executive Vice President of Information Systems and Global Services at Lockheed Martin, Linda Gooden attended SDSU after receiving her undergraduate degree in computer science at Youngstown State University. She joined Lockheed Martin in 1980 and from 1997 to 2006 was President of Lockheed Martin Information Technology (LMIT). Linda has numerous recognitions for her professional and community work and in 2005 was awarded an honorary doctorate at the University of Maryland. She retired in 2013.

Johnnie Williams

Born and raised in Southeast San Diego during the Great Depression, Johnnie Williams enrolled in City College and SDSU (last attended in 1977). In 1952 he joined the city police department and progressed from beat cop to being assigned to Burglary and next becoming a Homicide detective, some of whose cases were mentioned in mystery magazines and some were studied in classrooms as textbook cases. He died in 2010.

Keith Mikell

Artist Keith Mikell attended SDSU in the late 1970s and also the Otis Parsons College of Art and Design. His works have been exhibited at the Agora Gallery and the Lucy Florence Gallery in Los Angeles and they have been seen on the sets of numerous television sitcoms. The work on the right is titled "Benevolent Offering".

Hodari Adbul-Ali

A native San Diegan, Hodari Abdul-Ali spent two years at SDSU then transferred to Howard University where he graduated magna cum laud and was editor of the student newspaper, *The Hilltop*. In 1976 he formed Liberation Information Distributing Company, a wholesaler of reading materials concerning persons of African descent and Islam. Five years later he founded Pyramid Books in

Washington, DC. which became the first black-owned bookstore chain in the nation. In 1995 he opened Dar Es Salaam Book/Health Center in a Maryland suburb. Well known as a social activist who received many recognitions for his contributions and leadership of community and human rights groups, he also hosted "The Struggle Continues!" on radio station WPFW 89.3 FM. Surrounded by his wife, he died of cancer on April 30, 2011.

Karen Ruth Bass

From 1971 to 1973, U.S. Congresswoman Karen Bass attended SDSU majoring in philosophy. A Democrat, she was elected to the California State Assembly in 2004 representing the 47the District and from 2008 to 2010 served as Speaker of the California State Assembly and is proud of the 17 bills she sponsored that became law, especially those dealing with health insurance and foster care. In 2010 she was elected to the U.S. House of Representatives from California's 33rd Congressional District encompassing the Los Angeles enclaves of Ladera Heights, Baldwin Hills, and Culver City. A stalwart supporter of President Obama, in 2008 she was a co-chair of his California presidential campaign. She serves on the house Budget and Foreign Affairs Committees.

Willie J. Horton Jr.

A lifelong resident of San Diego, Willie Horton taught life sciences classes in elementary schools, was principal at two schools, and has sat on the boards of several academic and civic groups such as the San Diego Zoological Society, San Diego Youth Symphony, Urban League, SDSU Alumni, and Kappa Alpha Psi Fraternity. Among his recognitions are the Award for Outstanding Achievement in Education from National University and the Trailblazer in Education Award from the National Association of Negro Business and Professional Women's Club of San Diego.

Terry Price

Terry Price With a degree in public administration from SDSU (Class of '73), Terry Price has been a manager and general manager of several California businesses, including Carey Limousine, Bauer's Transportation, Avis Rent-A-Car. In 2011 he was franchise Owner and operator at A & B Trans Service, LLC/dba Budget Car and Truck Rental.

1970'S PROFILES

Sylvia Gayle Dayton Jones

Sylvia Gayle Dayton-Jones A graduate in the Class of '79, Dayton earned her Ph.D. in mass communications at Howard University in 1989. Today she is a businesswoman in the Washington D.C. area.

Dorothy L. Vails-Weber

A counselor at SDSU since 1970, Dr. Vails-Weber was quite active in the A.M.E. Church. She retired in 1998. In 2002 she co-founded and was president of Savant Development Inc. Management Consulting Services.

Errol Roy Seaton

Errol R. Seaton completed his Ph.D. dissertation on T.S. Eliot at UC-San Diego in 1977. After many years working in academic advising at SDSU, in 2005 he became a lecturer in the liberal studies department at Western Washington University teaching British and American literature. Between 1983 and 1988 he contributed twenty book reviews pertaining literature to the *San Diego Union* and the San Diego *Tribune*.

Peter H. Henson

Retired Air Force Lt. Col. Peter Henson, the son and nephew of distinguished SDSU athletes and military men Harold T. Henson and Allison M Henson, graduated from the university along with his sister, Tanja, in 1976. After receiving his master's degree in clinical psychology at the California School of Professional Psychology he entered the Air Force in 1981 to commence a career as a bomber navigator (B-52), instructor, and administrator. In retirement since 2003 he has worked as the administrative pastor on the staff of Eagle's Nest Worship Center in Omaha, Nebraska.

James King

Cuyamaca College track coach James King (formerly a coach at Grossmont College, San Diego City College, and San Diego Mesa College) was an SDSU hurdler who won the 400 meter event at the Pan American Games in 1975 and for several years was ranked among the nation's ten best hurdlers. For many years he held the world's records for men over age 40.

Kevin Edward Chaney

Kevin Edward Chaney The women's head basketball coach at University of Nebraska-Kearney from 2010 to 2016 was Kevin Chaney (Class of '79) who today is university counselor at Grand Canyon University. Kevin, who also has a master's degree in sports management from Southern Illinois University-Edwardsville, was formerly on the Board of Directors for the California Community College Women's Basketball Association.

Hilton I. Hale

In 2015 Hilton J. Hale published his self-help book *Get Free for Free: Non Economic Solutions in a Tough Economic Situation* (Tate Publishing). The Class of '79 graduate, he is CEO of Hilton Hilton I. Hale & Associates, an insurance agency in Columbus, Ohio. He has won numerous awards for both his professional and community service activities.

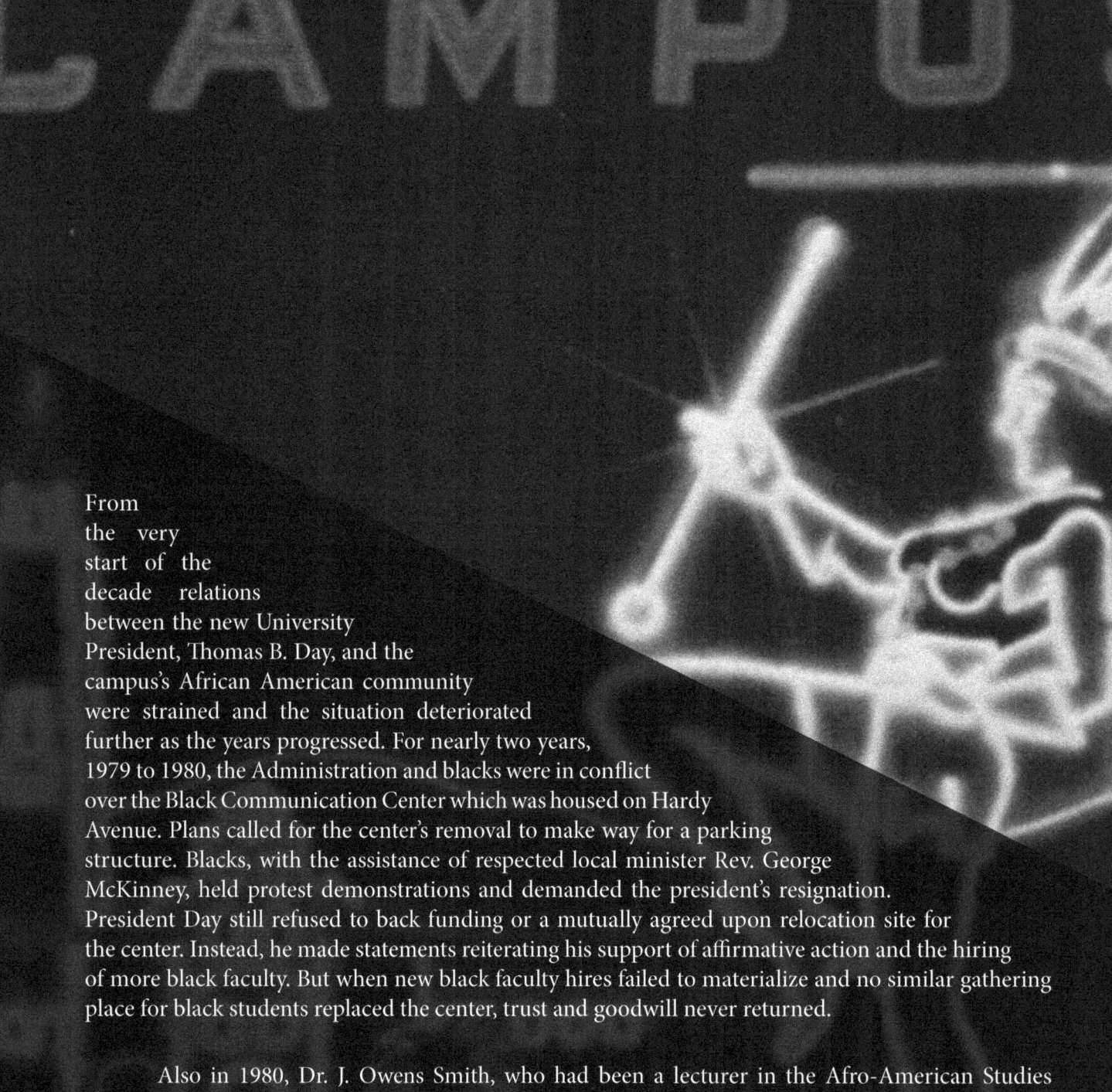

From the very start of the decade relations between the new University President, Thomas B. Day, and the campus's African American community were strained and the situation deteriorated further as the years progressed. For nearly two years, 1979 to 1980, the Administration and blacks were in conflict over the Black Communication Center which was housed on Hardy Avenue. Plans called for the center's removal to make way for a parking structure. Blacks, with the assistance of respected local minister Rev. George McKinney, held protest demonstrations and demanded the president's resignation. President Day still refused to back funding or a mutually agreed upon relocation site for the center. Instead, he made statements reiterating his support of affirmative action and the hiring of more black faculty. But when new black faculty hires failed to materialize and no similar gathering place for black students replaced the center, trust and goodwill never returned.

Also in 1980, Dr. J. Owens Smith, who had been a lecturer in the Afro-American Studies department, filed a class action discrimination complaint on behalf of black faculty and staff with the U.S. Labor Department's Office of Federal Contract Compliance Programs (OFCCP). OFCCP's compliance review in 1983 confirmed what many had suspected, that "SDSU made no special efforts to recruit blacks or any minority group."[52] Smith had applied for tenure tack status which his department had recommended. A similar situation had occurred with Smith's predecessor, Dr. Maulana Karenga, who in 1977 filed a grievance because an extension of his lectureship, approved by his department, was denied by the Administration. Smith charged that his efforts in defending black staff who had filed complaints was the cause of retaliation against him.

1980'S

1983 was a particularly disastrous year for blacks' relations with the Administration. First, a study released by the Chancellor's Office showed that in fact the number of black professors and support staff has dropped significantly both in terms of numbers and percentages, and that there were fewer such blacks on campus than when President Day arrived in 1978. The OFCCP detailed 15 areas of deficiency in the university's affirmative action program and recommended corrective measures to alleviate some "deep and severe" problems.[53] In its follow-up review in 1989, the Western Association of Schools and Colleges (WASC) put the campus on notice when it declared that:

> ...the University's affirmative action office does not have to have the resources to take a more aggressive leadership role and that its influence is little felt at all levels where appointments are made and retention is negotiated....The Affirmative Action Program for recruitment of students and its outcome are puzzling. We would expect, from the demographic data reviewed in the team meeting room, a marked increase in the number of minority students enrolled at SDSU. But such is not the case.[54]

An incident in 1983 which infuriated blacks was an interview with President Day's affirmative action coordinator, Robert McCabe, printed in an October issue of *The Daily Aztec* in which he said past "overzealous enforcement of the (equal opportunity) guidelines had led to reverse discrimination"; that "protected-group members who are less qualified than their competitors" had been hired; and that, "much of affirmative action is creating a social problem."[55] The majority of the university's tenured black faculty members responded with a letter to McCabe challenging his qualifications to hold his position. They charged that he had "created an impression that hiring blacks and other minorities has required the university to abandon reasonable personnel standards and principles of fairness," and that his remarks displayed "an incredible insensitivity, and perhaps even hostility towards affirmative action."[56] They also demanded that McCabe either resign or be fired and they refocused their anger at President Day.

In early May 1984, a two-part series appeared in *The Daily Aztec* which examined the school's affirmative action record. It concluded: "After almost nine years of affirmative action, SDSU…has actually lost ground in the hiring of black faculty. Figures from the Department of Labor show that, from 1975, when affirmative action began, to 1981, the number of black faculty decreased from 23 to 19."[57] Statistics also revealed that of 84 tenure track positions filled from 1981 to 1983, only one was filled with an African American. Twice between 1982 and 1986 the U.S. Department of Labor was called in to investigate complaints of racial discrimination and harassment of black faculty and staff, and such complaints grew dramatically toward the end of the decade as blacks felt disillusioned and without a sympathetic ear in the Administration.

There were occasional instances of racist graffiti and racist hate literature on campus. In 1987, Kasimu Harley, a Student Resource Center employee, was reported by *The Daily Aztec* to have torn down a poster on campus on which a white fraternity advertised a "slave auction" for members who would "sell" their services as a fundraiser; and a year later another white fraternity timed their "Rasta Night" party to coincide with Black History Month, which met with protest. In 1983, psychology major Veronica Hawkins was arrested and allegedly manhandled by three male campus policemen who thought she had tried illegally to resale a textbook. She sent President Day an unexpected Valentine's Day gift: a greeting card attached to a bouquet of roses with a summons enclosed informing him the university was being sued for false arrest, assault and battery, etc.

More significant, however, was the founding of the Study Commission on Black Affairs (SCOBA) in 1985. The group initially intended only to "study" the problems blacks encountered and to "advise" those in authority, but as dissatisfaction with the Administration escalated, and as more grievances were filed and too few black faculty and staff hired, SCOBA was transformed, becoming move assertive and vocal about a worsening situation. After examining some disturbing data on black hiring, SCOBA co-chairs Gwen Patrick-Buie and Harold Brown (a library staff worker and an administrator) wrote President Day on March 8, 1988 mildly suggesting reforms to help the university's affirmative action effort. Instead of an accommodating reply, they got what seemed to them a defensive reaction to their concerns. Though stunned and disappointed by the response, they arranged for a series of meetings with the president in 1988 and 1989 hoping that dialogue would lead to something positive. They were mistaken. A volcano of pent-up anger and outrage was about to erupt—and erupt it did.

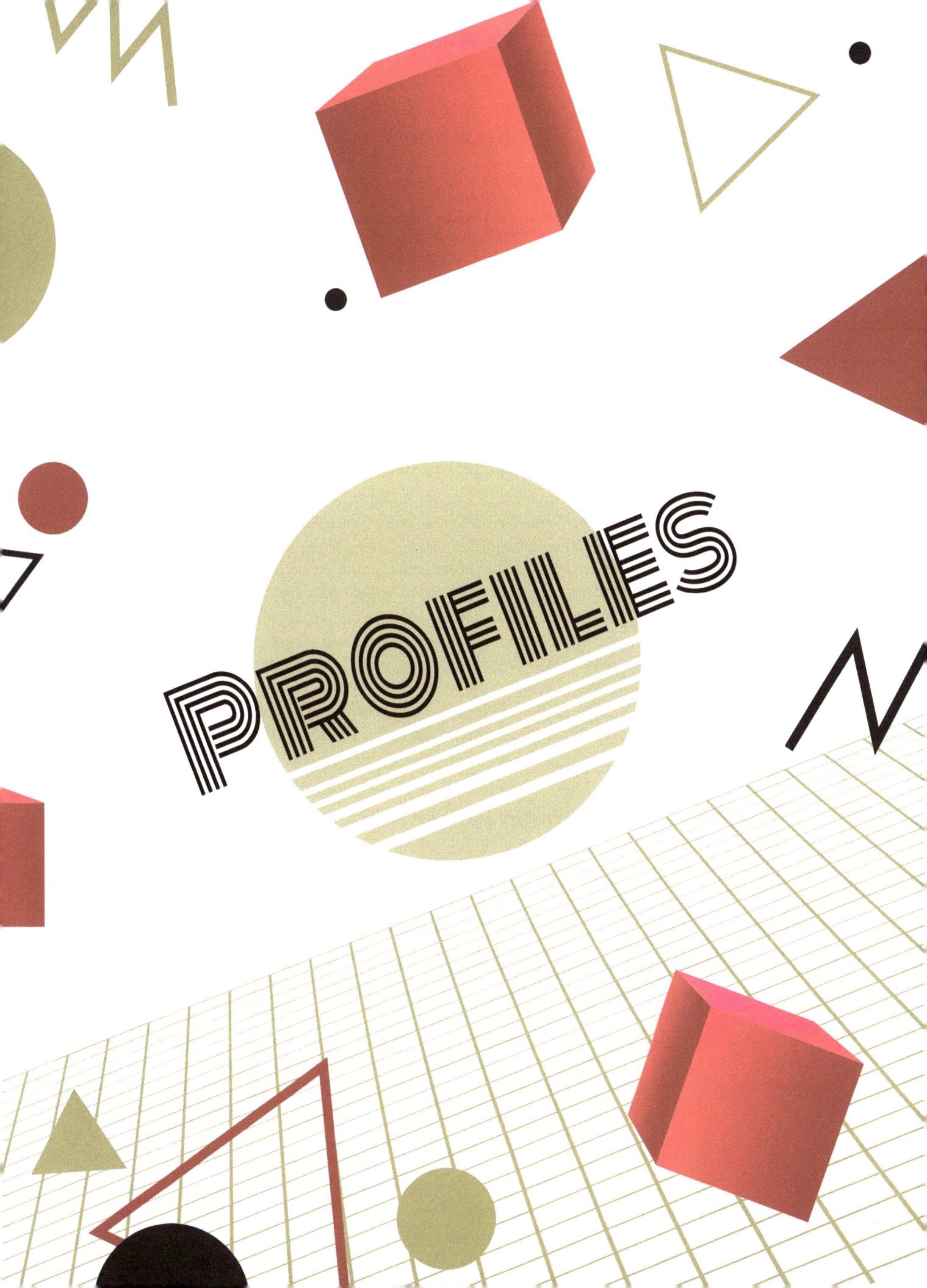

Michael Jerome Cage: NBA Standout

At 6 feet 9 inches, Michael Cage set scoring and basketball rebounding records at SDSU. He was drafted by the Los Angeles Clippers in 1984 and later played on NBA teams in Seattle, Philadelphia, Cleveland, and New Jersey. In 1988, Cage was the NBA's rebounding champion averaging 13.03 points per game. In a recent interview he stated: "My last game of the season at San Diego State: They retired my jersey while I was still active, and that meant a lot to me. I worked hard as a student athlete and that was a special honor." Cage was TV analyst for the Memphis Grizzlies pro basketball team. His home state honored him by inducting Cage in the Arkansas Hall of Fame.

Lena Nozizwe Siwundhla: Star Reporter

Emmy and Golden Mike Award-winning television news correspondent Lena Nozizwe Siwundhla (Class of `80), better known as Lena Nozizwe, has crisscrossed the globe investigating and reporting on high-profile stories. Starting out on local radio station KFMB AM/FM and Channel 8 KFMB-TV and she rose to national attention as a regular correspondent for the Fox TV weekly show "America's Most Wanted" and as a reporter and commentator for media giants CBS, ESPN, and BET. Nozizwe, who was born in a village in Malawi, owns a production company called Malume Media. Her book, *Starring in Your Own Life*, was published by Simon and Schuster in 2001. She has taught communication classes at SDSU as a part-time instructor.

Derek W. Cotton: Champion Fencer

Winner of the 1986 Southern California Collegiate Fencing League competition, Derek Cotton (Class of '87,'93) was a member of the Stanford Fencing Club 1995 U.S. Men's Foil National Championship Team, and was a back-to-back winner of Pacific Coast Sabre titles. Well know as a fencing coach and as a fencing competition referee, he was the only American selected to referee at the 2000 Olympic Games in Sydney, Australia and the 2004 Games in Athens, Greece. Cotton was the co-founder of SDSU's fencing team. From 2002 to 2005 he was the owner and head coach of the Los Angeles Fencer's Club. He was a board member of the U.S. Fencing Association (2004-2008) while at his day jobs worked as recruiting manager for Farmer's Insurance and other firms. He lives in Los Angeles.

1980'S PROFILES

Carroll Parrott Blue: Award-Winning Filmmaker

An outstanding documentary filmmaker and a professor of communication at SDSU since 1984, Blue is a board member and Media Chair of The California Council for the Humanities. Her film "Conversations with Roy DeCarava" was Blue Ribbon Winner at the 1984 American Film Festival and Second Prize Winner at the Black American Cinema Awards. Blue was also a segment producer in 1992 for the award-winning PBS series "Eyes on the Prize." The publication of her book and accompanying CD in 2003 titled *The Dawn at My Back: A Memoir of a Black Texas Memoir, 1900-2000* (University of Texas Press) was warmly received by acclaimed historians and others and won a jury award at the 2004 Sundance Film Festival. She is presently a research professor at the University of Houston's Center for Public History and the Texas Learning & Computation Center, and she directs her non-profit organization, The Dawn Project, that promotes community development through the use of skilled media production and distribution by citizens. One of her television programs was on "NOVA" ("Mystery of the Senses: Vision"). She was appointed a World Academy of Art and Science Fellow in 2007.

Marvin Vernell Curtis: Pres. Clinton's Choir Director and Composer

A part-timer in the Africana Studies department in the late 1980s, Curtis, a Julliard alumnus, revitalized, toured, and directed SDSU's Black Gospel Choir (named best campus organization of 1986) and directed other choirs and orchestras around town. He left to get his doctorate at the University of the Pacific; taught at Cal State Stanislaus; was director of President Clinton's 1992 Inauguration Choir for which he was commissioned to composed a special piece (the first African American thus commissioned); was Assistant Dean of the College of Humanities and Social Sciences and Choral Director at Fayetteville State University; and in 2007 he was one of 26 fellows for the American Association of State Colleges and Universities' (AASCU) Millennium Leadership Initiative. He assumed the Deanship of the Ernestine M. Raclin School of the Arts at Indiana University South Bend on August 1, 2008.

OTHER 1980'S NOTABLES

Barron McCall

The Barron McCall Scholarship was launched by Alpha Phi Alpha fraternity in memory of Barron McCall, an admired fraternity brother and SDSU graphic arts major who was killed in an automobile accident in 1987. The "Gospel Extravaganza" was held annually by the fraternity to raise money for the fund which is distributed to from two to four students each year.

Susan Love Brown

Graduating in the Class of '87, Brown next got her Ph.D. at UC San Diego and today is Professor of Anthropology at Florida Atlantic University. Her book is titled *Intentional Community: An Anthropological Perspective* (SUNY Press, 2002).

Nelda F. Farrington

Nelda F. Farrington In 1988, Nelda Farrington (Class of '89), then a 22-year-old journalism major, was crowned Miss Virgin Islands. She said she had mastered a technique for "competitive smiling" and went to the Miss Universe Contest in Taiwan that year. She later owned two businesses and became chairperson of the British Virgin Islands Chamber of Commerce and worked in film production at Universal Studios for a number of years before returning home.

Lei-Chala Wilson

Working as a public defender in San Diego, Wilson (Class of '85), with a law degree from UC-Davis, in the year 2000 became President of the California Association of Black Lawyers, a group representing 5,000 African American attorneys throughout the state. She has also served as president of the Earl B. Gilliam Bar Association, representing black attorneys in San Diego, and for several years was president of the local branch of the NAACP.

1980'S PROFILES

Shikana Temille Porter

Currently Director of Counseling Services at Whittier College, Dr. Porter (Class of '80) was previously Director of Disability Services & Programs at the University of Southern California. She had also worked as a lecturer at SDSU. She is also a clinical psychologist in private practice.

Bobbie J. Atkins

Dr. Atkins, who has received numerous honors and taught in the College of Education since 1989 is, among other things, National Coordinator of the Rehabilitation Services Administration's Rehabilitation Cultural Diversity Initiative. She is a Certified Rehabilitation Counselor (CRC). Named in her honor, the Bobbie J. Atkins Rehabilitation Research Award "is given annually by the National Association for Multicultural Rehabilitation Concerns."

Charles Neal

A former Colorado policeman, Charles Neal worked in EOP at SDSU since 1981. He holds five college degrees, including a master's degree in counseling-psychology from SDSU (Class of '83). It was Neal who first had the idea to launch the African American Scholarship Fund which he co-founded with Wanda Clay Majors (EOP) and Dr. JoAnne Cornwell (Africana Studies).

Martin Moss

Head coach of the football team at San Diego Mesa College since 1992, Martin Moss, a Lincoln High and UCLA graduate, earned his master's degree in counseling at SDSU (Class of '87). He also has a master's degree in education from National University.

La Tanya M. Sheffield

Winner of the 1988 NCAA 400 meter hurdles, LaTanya Sheffield (Class of `86) was also a1988 Olympics finalist in that event. Today she is a motivational speaker, a mother of two children, and organizer of the annual LaTanya Sheffield Sporting Clinic in Tucson, Arizona, and is a contact for the nonprofit Sports Extravaganza.

Peter Alfred Dual

The first full dean of African descent at SDSU was Dr. Peter A. Dual who served as Dean of the College of Health & Human Services from 1983 to 1993. He left to become Vice President for Academic Affairs at Cal Poly Pomona and later held the same post at Eastern Washington University, resigning in 2002. In his memory the NCCEP/GEAR UP established the Dr. Peter A. Dual International Fellowship Program. He died in North Las Vegas, Nevada on August 11, 2010.

Cameron Gary

Holder of a 3rd Degree Black Belt in Aikido and a 1st Degree Black Belt in Jujutsu, Gary (Class of '84) is a California peace officer who has an instructor ranking from the FBI. He has taught at the San Diego police academy (including SWAT), the Conway Academy of Martial Arts, and briefly at SDSU. Gary has also been a track coach at Helix High and Monte Vista High. He owns a physical conditioning and a martial art business.

Mshinda Nyofu

Mshinda Kyofu (a.k.a. Glenn Kevin Grigsby), Class of '85, is an experienced community activist; leader in the local chapters of US and BAPAC; was legislative representative in the Office of State Senator Steve Peace, 40th District; and worked on the staffs of two 4th District City Councilmen. He teaches social studies in schools in Houston, Texas.

Angela Lynn Hudson

An assistant professor of nursing at UCLA, Angela L. Hudson (Class of `86, `93) earned her Ph.D. at UC San Francisco in 1999. Previously, she taught nursing at Cal State-Fresno.

Joan Sabrina Mims-Cox

Dr. Joan Mims-Cox (M.A., Class of '87) is Professor of Education Cal State-Los Angeles where she is also Director of the Los Angeles Accelerated Schools Center and Coordinator of the Bilingual Program. Fluent in Spanish, she has co-authored several textbooks in English and Spanish.

Winnie O. Willis

Dr. Willis Professor of Public Health in the Graduate School of Public Health (GSPH). Employed at SDSU in 1984, she became Director of the GSPH Institute for Public Health (IPH), and retired in 2004.

Carolena L. Lyons-Lawrence

From 1987 to 2004 Carolena Lyons-Lawrence was a professor of Information and Decision Systems. One of her scholarly articles, "Integrating Writing and Negotiation Skills," was published in *Business Communication Quarterly*, in June 2002.

Charles Clifford Shockley

The nation's first black corporate pilot (Philip Morris Inc.) and a former president of the local chapter of the Tuskegee Airmen Inc., Dr. Charles Shockley joined the staff of the SDSU Foundation in 1982. He headed the Minority Business Development Center and was later program director of Defense Conversion Center at the Foundation until he left in 2001. In 1994, Shockley was honored for his work in assisting minorities in business and commerce with the Economic Parity Award, presented by the Joint Conference Inc.

David Harrison Butler

A former military officer during the Vietnam War, Dr. Butler was a full professor in the accounting faculty. He was employed from 1981 to 2002.

Darryl L. White

Known for his work in devising strategies to educate African American males, Darryl White (Class of '85) became the principal of two high schools in Sacramento: Grant High and Thurgood Marshall/Sarah Jones High.

Aaron Thigpen

A certified lifeguard and scuba diver, Aaron Thigpen (photo left, Class of '87) became the head basketball coach and a physical education instructor at Chabot College in Hayward, California. He owns Gamespeed, an athletic performance company in Dublin, California. He continues to compete in track races.

Charles A. Sippial, Jr.

A former U.S. Air Force colonel who worked at the Pentagon, Charles Sippial was Director of Physical Plant from 1989 to 1995. He left for Texas A&M University to be its vice president for administration.

Ella Fay Sloan

Professor of Cosmetology at San City College who retired in 2006, Ella F. Sloan received her bachelor's and master's degree from SDSU and a doctorate in education at the University of San Diego in 2002. In 1997 she established the W.E.B. DuBois Leadership Institute for Young Scholars, focused on 4th through 8th-grade students; and was active in the local NAACP and the George L. Stevens Senior Center, serving both groups as treasurer. She arranged student travels to West Africa that brought school supplies to Ashanti village children in Kumasi, Ghana.

Ezequiel Fory Palacios

A native of Colombia (an Afro-Colombian), Dr. Palacios taught in the Mexican American Studies department from 1972 to 1984. He later taught at the Escuela de Trabajo Social de Tijuana (School of Social Work in Tijuana), Autonomous University of Baja California.

Jane B. Milligan

Jane B. Milligan A poet and high school special education teacher, Jane Milligan (Class of '87, '00) received two of her academic three degrees from SDSU. She is a co-founder of the African America writers and Artists of San Diego and a published poet who has read her works in San Diego and New York City.

1980'S PROFILES

Jason C.K. Ekwena

Jason Ekwena, M.D. (Class of '82) earned his medical degree at the University of Santiago (Chile). He is an internist board certified in family medicine practicing in Urbandale, Iowa.

Chistopher Karlton Gwynn

Christopher Karlton Gwynn The brother of Tony Gwynn, Chris represented SDSU on the 1984 Olympic baseball team. Between 1987 and 1996 he played with the San Diego Padres, the Kansas City Royals, and the Los Angeles Dodgers (seven seasons). He was the Director of Player Personnel for the Padres in 2011, then Director of Player Development for the Seattle Mariners.

Lynor E. Holt Jackson-Marks

A part-time lecturer at Loma Linda University and supervisor/program manager at the Institute for Black Parenting in Riverside, Jackson-Marks (Class of '86) was the western liaison for the National Association of Perinatal Social Workers. She has a doctorate in educational psychology

Wanda Clay Majors

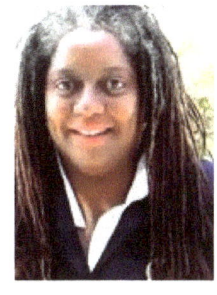

Coordinator of SOAR and the EOP mentoring program at SDSU, Wanda Clay Majors received her master's degree in education at SDSU. Her work in the community has included leadership roles in the YMCA and the Community Economic Development Corporation (CEDA), and she is a co-founder of the Golden ANKH Association assisting the positive development of black teens attending high school.

Ernest Riggins

Arriving at SDSU in 1983 as head coach of the women's basketball team, Riggins (photo left) had an impressive winning record when he left in 1989.

Derek Cannon

Jazz trumpeter Derek Cannon (Class of '89) has performed with such great entertainers as Natalie Cole, The Four Tops, Clark Terry, and The Temptations and has managed to teach part-time at Grossmont College. From 1995 to 1999 he chaired the Jazz Studies department at Chicago State University. Cannon, who is also a composer and has a number of recordings to his credit, has performed at top jazz festivals in Europe and the Americas. His recent recording include "Free Your Mind" with Walter Beasley in 2009 and "Destiny" with Kamau Kenyatta in 2007. In addition to his position as studio artist teacher (jazz trumpet) he is Director of Jazz Studies and co-Chair of the Music department at Grossmont College. In 2014 he was Department Chair & Director of Jazz & Afro-Cuban Studies. In 2010 he recorded "Coup d' Eclat" with Monette Marino and "From Me To You" with Paula Prophet, and in 2009 "Free Your Mind" with Walter Beasely.

JoAnne Jenkins Cornwell

A professor of French and Africana Studies since 1984, Dr. Cornwell is also an entrepreneur who owns Sisterlocks, a trademark operation that promotes African hair braiding and has certified trainers in seven states. In 1999, her lawsuit against the California Board of Barbering and Cosmetology attracted national attention and the case was decided in her favor in a federal district court.

Sophia Angeli Nelson

In 1996, Sophia Nelson (Class of '89), a political science major at SDSU, won the Republican nomination for Congress from the 1st District of New Jersey but was forced to withdraw because of illness. A conservative Republican, she is an attorney who has worked as an investigative counsel with the House Government Reform and Oversight Committee.

Derrick Monroe

A 1986 graduate of SDSU, Monroe was the operations manager of the new Encinitas Community and Senior Center, an currently is Community Center Manager, City of Encinitas.

1980'S PROFILES

Perette Godwin

Having worked with nonprofit groups and having been a DJ for jazz radio station KSDS in San Diego, Godwin (Class of '85), a journalism major, ventured into television new broadcasting and became a news anchor and reporter for KYMA-TV in Yuma, Arizona, then at KSWB-TV and Fox 5 in San Diego. In 2014 she worked as a publicist for Scatena Daniels Communications and was a freelance reporter for San Diego's XETV. In 2015, having served for six years on the SDSU Alumni Association Board of Advisors, she became president of the board. Presently, senior community relations specialist at California Coast Credit Union, she is a PTA president and volunteer with the San Diego Music Foundation

Millie Robinson

Innovative EOP counselor and teacher Mildred "Millie" Robinson (Class of '82, '89) is a certified diversity trainer who has worked in various departments on aspects of student outreach, academic assistance, tutoring, and access services.

Tesfaye W. Leka

Tesfaye W. Leka A medical doctor with the Harrison Jones Medical Group in Long Beach, California, Dr. Leka (Class of `85) practices in internal medicine.

Dennis T. Gibson

Mr. Gibson has recently served as San Diego County Assistant Tax Collector. Prior to this, from 2005 to 2007 he was Ballpark Administrator for the City of San Diego, the city's Water Department's CFO/Business Operations Manager, Supervising Financial Management Analyst and senior policy advisor to the Mayor. In 2014 he was the county's Assistant Treasurer-Tax Collector.

Yayesh Lissane

Mr. Lissane (Class of '84) is president of Ethiopian Community of San Diego Inc. whose mission is to aid Ethiopian refugees and students in adjusting to life here. A computer science graduate, he has worked at the Salk Institute, HD Supply, and NetHere Inc.

Francheska Ahmed-Cawthorne

Author of *Sista, Girlfren' Breaks It Down…When Mom's Not Around* (1996) published by Fireside Books/Simon & Schuster, Ahmed-Cawthorne (Class of `86) was married to local Channel 10 newsman Herb Cawthorne.

Percy Ellis

Percy Ellis (class of '81), Professor of Information Techology at Yuba College, is also a certified Microsoft and Novell systems engineer.

Webster Slaughter

Drafted by the Cleveland Browns in 1986, wide receiver Webster Slaughter played for 13 years with 5 team in the NFL. He also played in the 1990 Pro Bowl.

Theophilus B.A. Addo

A native of Ghana, Dr. Addo (photo left) is Associate Professor of Management Information Systems. A Monty awardee who has won a number of outstanding teacher and faculty awards, he has been a member of the Academic Senate and has taught at SDSU since 1987.

Asfaw Beyene

Dr. Beyene is Professor of Mechanical Engineering, graduate advisor, and director of SDSU's Industrial Assessment Center which is funded by the U.S. Department of Energy. He has published nearly 40 papers on energy efficiency.

June Edmonds

June Edmonds (Class of '82), a painter, printmaker, and public artist, has exhibited her work in galleries across the state and has taught at the Academy of Visual and Performing Arts in Culver, California, Cerritos College, and the public school system.

1980'S PROFILES

Michael Brunker

For several years in the 1980s Michael Brunker was an assistant basketball coach under Smokey Gaines. Since 1997, he has been the very successful executive director of the Jackie Robinson YMCA in Southeast San Diego.

David Bradley

Novelist David Bradley taught in the English department during the 1980-81 school year while putting the finishing touches on *The Chaneysville Incident* (Harper & Row, 1981), winner of the coveted PEN/Faulkner Prize in 1982.

Floyd Windom Hayes, III

Floyd Windom Hayes, III. Author of three books and many articles, political scientist Dr. Floyd Hayes worked in the Africana Studies department from 1986 to 1992. He currently teaches at Johns Hopkins University.

Karen Rostodha-Bonner

Host and producer of the KPBS-TV show "Full Focus," Karen Rostodha (Class of '86) reported the news and anchored television news at stations in California and Texas. She followed stories as far away as Japan. Rostodha, a San Diego native, won honors in 1999, including the Edward R. Murrow Award for Best Spot News, for her feature on the "Salinas Standoff." Two other notable blacks who worked as producers and show hosts at KPBS-TV were Alice Almeta Speaks in the 1970s and Anasa Briggs in the 1980s.

Sha' Givens

Founder of Success Works, Sha' Givens (Class of '85) is a motivational speaker and a Christian evangelist who talks to prisoners, high school students, and religious groups across the country. Her novel titled *Through the Storm* (2002) is about the friendship and religious journey of two women.

Michael Edward Thomas

A drama major, actor Michael Thomas (Class of '85) has appeared in several Hollywood movies, various commercials, and highly rated television shows like "Will & Grace" and "Melrose Place."

Melake Ghebrehiwet

His Ph.D. thesis at U.S.I.U. was on the political history of Ethiopia, but Dr. Melake Ghebrehiwet (Class of '80, '95) works as a senior project manager for the San Diego County Parks and Recreation Department.

Reginald S. Blaylock

A former star lineman on the Aztec football team, Reggie Blaylock (Class of '88) decided against a career in the NFL and became Associate Athletic Director at SDSU and, later, Director of the Office of Student Recruiting and School Relations and Director of EOP and Ethnic Affairs. With an education doctorate from SDSU, in 2013 he was promoted to Associate Vice President for Student Services.

Rodney E. Van

An exceptional long jumper on the Aztec track team in the late 1980s, Rodney Van (Class of '88) became a probation officer and head track and field coach at Monte Vista High. He is the owner of VanSports, a sporting goods store in Spring Valley and is a track Coach at Steele Canyon High School

Chet Carney

Anyone who regularly attends Aztecs sporting events is familiar with Chet Carney (Class of '86), known as "SDSU's No.1 Fan." With his trademarks red hardhat and overalls, and turning cartwheels, this chucky ball of energy and enthusiasm paces the aisles inspiring the crowd to push the team to victory. Carney was actually a former member of the SDSU cheerleading squad. He is an employee of the city of San Diego.

1980'S PROFILES

James Collins

In 1999, James Collins (Class of `85) was named head athletic trainer for the San Diego Chargers. With two decades of experience with teams in the National Football League, Collins also is a member of the NFL Safety Panel.

Theodore W. O'Neal

At age 82 Theodore "Ted" McNeil (Class of '82) became one of the oldest students ever to graduate from SDSU. He died May 18, 1992 at age 88. A former union leader in Illinois, he was a past president of the San Diego NAACP.

Barron Jodell Peeler

As one of the finest gospel singers around, Barron Peeler (Class of `88) has song with award-winning gospel groups and appeared on stage with such well known singers as the late James Cleveland, Take 6, Brian McKnight, Walter Hawkins, Little Richard, Shirley Caesar, Chante Moore, Larnell Harris, etc. His album titled "Pressin On," first released on the Chapel/Bridge label in 1998, has been re-released. Peeler's master's degree in public health was earned at SDSU. His album "Journey of Life" was released in 2007.

Relda Robertson-Beckley

Receiving her M.P.H. at SDSU in 1989, Relda Robertson-Beckley acquired her doctorate in public health at UC Berkeley. She has taught nursing classes at San Francisco State University and Samuel Merritt College and has been employed by the California Department of Heath Services.

Chana Perry

She was on the U.S. Basketball Writers Association's All-American Team in 1989 and name one of the 10 players on the Kodak All-American Team that year. Averaging 23.5 points and 13.1 rebounds per game, 6 foot 5 inch Chana Perry led the 1989 women's basketball team under coach Ernest Riggins (see above) to a 25-9 record season.

Lloyd G. Cato

A former Associated Students vice president, Lloyd Cato is Vice President of Merchant Enablement & Information Management. He was formerly Director of PC Development at American Express. Cato earned his B.A. at SDSU in 1989 and later received his M.B.A. at Arizona State University.

Daniel E. Walker

After being granted his Ph.D. in history (with distinction) in 2000 at the University of Houston, Daniel E. Walker (Class of '89), a former Associated Students president, published the highly praised book *No More, No More: Slavery and Cultural Resistance in Havana and New Orleans* (University of Minnesota Press, 2004). A lecturer in Ethnic Studies at UC-Riverside, he has also taught at Indiana University and Occidental College. He has received numerous grants, fellowships, scholarships and awards mainly for his academic, photographic, film, music, and archival project pertaining to African American history and culture. In 2010 he was Director of Research and Archive Development for the Gospel Music History Archive at the University of Southern California. He is President/CEO of Perfect Works, a multimedia idea and history research firm.

Henry A. Alvarez III

With considerable experience in public housing, Mr. Alvarez (Class of '83), an Afro-American Studies major, in 2004 became President and CEO of the San Antonio Housing Authority. In 2005, representing the National Association of Housing and Redevelopment Officials (NAHRO), he testified before a Congressional subcommittee on housing and community opportunity and lobbied Congress to aid victims of Hurricane Katrina. In 2007 he was hailed as one of the top ten public housing experts in the nation. In 2014 he was executive director of the San Francisco Housing Authority.

Joseph Johnson

2003 Monty Award recipient Dr. Joseph Johnson (Class of '82), SDSU's QUALCOMM Professor of Educational Leadership, is the founding president of the National Association for the Education of Homeless Children and Youth. In 2005 he was made executive director of the National Center for Urban School

Janice Eurana Jackson

Formerly an Assistant Professor of Communication Sciences and Disorders at the University of South Carolina, Dr. Janice Jackson (Class of '84, '87) wrote her Ph.D. thesis at the University of Massachusetts at Amherst in 1998. She sat on the advisory board of the National Association for the Education of African American Children with Learning Disabilities.

Kerwin J. Danley

A native of Los Angeles, Kerwin Joseph Danley was an Aztec baseball teammate of the legendary Tony Gwynn. A sociology major while at SDSU, he commenced his career as a professional baseball umpire in 1985 and by 1998 was working in the Major League. He has appeared in four Division Series, one American League Championship Series, and in the 2007 All-Star Game. Off the field, he is a board member of the Derek Kennard Foundation.

Taha Taha

A native of Sudan, Dr. Taha Taha (Class of '86) earned his master's degree here in public health then acquired his Ph.D. at Johns Hopkins University where today he works in the Bloomberg School of Public Heath as Professor and Co-Director of Infectious Disease Epidemiology. The author of numerous published studies on HIV/Aids, malaria, STDs, microbicides and antiretrovirals, he has received several prestigious awards and fellowships.

Rodney Knox

Nike Inc. Director of Communications for Team Sports is Rodney Knox who has worked in integrated sports marketing since 1981. With a speech and communications degree from SDSU and a master's degree in sports management from San Diego State University, he spent 19 years with the San Francisco 49ers as Director of Communications negotiating media deals and doing promotionals after a stint with the San Diego Charger. Rodney has also taught sports, media, and society at two universities.

Transformation. In 2012 he received the Local NAACP's Carter G. Woodson Award. In April 2014 he was made Dean of the School of Education at SDSU, having previously served as interim dean.

Rahn Sheffield

For four decades track coach Rahn Sheffield worked with the university's cross country and field athletes. Named head coach of the track program in 1991, during his tenure 78 students made it to NCAA championships, 25 competed in Olympics trials, 19 were tapped All-American, 4 became Olympic participants, and 3 won NCAA individual championships. Sheffield was three-time conference coach of the year and in 2003 he directed the team that garnered the Mountain West Conference outdoor title, defeating perennial champion Brigham Young University. An alumnus (Class of '80), he was a two-time All-American track star himself. Sheffield retired in December 2008. In 2013 he left to become assistant track coach (sprints and hurdles) at UC-Davis.

Stephen Sayles

The head athletic trainer for the Oakland A's pro baseball team from 2007 to 2010 was Stephen "Soup" Sayles (Class of '84). A former outfielder for a San Diego Padres minor league team, the Miami Marlins, in 1983 he suffered a shoulder injury that ended his pro career dream. He next worked as a trainer for the Padres' minor league team in Spokane, Washington, and later was a trainer for teams in Charleston, South Carolina, Wichita, Kansas, and Las Vegas before joining the A's in 1998. He was selected as one of two American League trainers for the 2009 All-Star Game. In 2014 he was a representative of Wealth Consulting Group. In Las Vegas.

Joes Lewis Fulcher, Jr.

A former school psychologist in the Sweetwater Union High School District and currently Chief Student Services Officer for the San Diego Unified School District, Dr. Joe L. Fulcher Jr. (Class of '88) received his doctorate at Claremont Graduate University/SDSU in 2003. In 2006 he was president of the Association of African-American Educators.

Pamela Elaine Pettit-Noel

University of Iowa social work professor Pamela E. Pettit-Noel, age 43, died at her family's home on February 10, 2008. Born in Compton, California, she was granted her MSW and MPH degrees at SDSU and her Ph.D. at the University of North Carolina. A specialist in child and maternal welfare issues, she was a foster parent to several children. Prof. Noel-Pettit had also been appointed by the

1980'S PROFILES

Governor to the Iowa Council for Early ACCESS, was active in her church, and a mentor to numerous students at the university.

Clarence Nunn

President and CEO of GE Capital Solutions Fleet Services business, Clarence Nunn graduated from SDSU with a degree in marketing and was granted his MBA at Rensselaer Polytechnic Institute. Prior to his present position this former defensive back for the New Orleans Saints worked in several areas of GE, including sales, global media and data storage, specialty products and services, plastics, and equipment financing. He has been awarded a US Patent for selecting product colors and has earned the Master Black Belt Certification.

Duke Windsor

Texas-born former U.S. Marine Duke Windsor studied voice at SDSU in 1985, sang in the San Diego Opera Chorus, became a 4th Dan Black Belt, an actor, bullrider, illustrator, architectural draftsman and editorial cartoon, but today he is best known as a first rate artist whose paintings have graced galleries across the country and in the U.K. His works have won awards at the San Diego County Fair and the California State Fair. He has also worked as an exhibit designer/preparator for the San Diego Museum of Art, the Museum of Photographic Arts, the Museum of Man, the San Diego Museum of Natural History, and the Mingei International Museum. In 2007 he was named Director of Exhibits and Lead Exhibit Designer for the USS Midway Museum.

Marsha R. Dodson

Marsha R. Dodson A contracting officer for the Naval Facilities Engineering Command Southwest, Marsha R. Dodson (Class of '84) has established an impressive list of achievements in community service, among them vice-chairman of Concerned Parents Alliance Inc. (Poway), chairperson of the educational component of College Bound San Diego, co-founder of Empowering Parents, and she is a member of Alpha Kappa Alpha Sorority Inc. An SDSU journalism graduate, Dodson received the 2007 Educator of the Year Award from the North County NAACP. The mother of three grown children, she is the co-author of *Empowering Parents: A Parent's Guide to Taking Control of Your Child's Educational Journey*.

Albert Dwayne Newman

An accounting major at SDSU, Albert "Newmie" Newman was on the All-Conference baseball team and a running back on the football team. He became a popular switch-hitting infielder for the Minnesota Twins and was a team coach from 1993 to 2005. Newman also played for the Montreal Expos and the Texas Rangers and was a scout for the Arizona Diamondbacks. But it was in Minnesota where he resides that he continues his community work through Newman Rewards LLC and where he hosts the "The Al Newman Show," radio 1280 AM, highlighting Minnesota sports.

A. Tobin

The son of a village chief and born and raised in Nigeria until 1982, Tobin, a successful local real estate company owner, is an SDSU alumnus (economics) and a graduate of the San Diego Police Academy. Four years in a row he was recognized as an "Outstanding Employee." He enjoys speaking to high school youth across the nation. Tobin has been awarded many honors for his business-related activities and has sold more than 300 homes since 1999 in San Diego and Riverside Counties.

Christopher Holden

Chis Holden (Class of '83) led the city of Pasadena, California as its first black mayor from 1997 to 1999, and has occupied a seat on the Pasadena City Council since 1989. A Democrat and the son of ex-Los Angeles City Councilman Nate Holden, in high school he was senior class president and was on the championship basketball team. He played four years on the Aztec basketball team and graduated with a business degree. He has served as an officer of the Burbank Airport Authority and pushed for Pasadena's drug-free zones and slumlord ordinance. In 2012 he was elected to the California State Assembly, representing the 41st District. Reelected in 2014, he was appointed Assistant Majority Floor Leader in the Assembly.

Arthur Boyd Jr.

Retiring after 23 years as a Navy Master Chief Petty Officer, Arthur Boyd returned to school to get his master's degree at SDSU (Class of '88) and a Ph.D. in education at La Salle University. Having previously worked at San Diego City College for sixteen years, presently he is employed as a counselor at San Diego Mesa College.

1980'S PROFILES

Michael D. Robinson

The Commanding Officer of the Marine Corps Security Group located in Quantico, Virginia, is SDSU alumnus Col. Michael D. Robinson (Class of '89) who received further education at Harvard University's Kennedy School of Government, Amphibious Warfare School, Marine Corps Command and Staff, and the Joint Forces Staff College. Col. Robinson has previous held military leadership posts in Korea, Iraq, Japan, and several American states including Company Commander, Weapons Training Battalion, Parris Island.

Gregory Wilson

Gregory Wilson While studying for his graduate degree in social work at SDSU in 1988, Gregory Wilson was recruited for a management trainee job in personnel. Now a seasoned professional in the field of human resource management, he has worked as Vice President of Hot Topic which at one time one of the fast growing companies of its kind in the world. He has also held top HR management positions at BSR, Private Equity Management, and Wal-Mart. In 2011, he was named one of the "Best HR Consultants" in Long Beach, California. He is a founding member of Senior Human Resource Professionals.

Nathaniel Buggs

With undergraduate and graduate degrees in public health from SDSU(Class of '89, '91), Nathaniel Buggs has worked for nearly two decades for San Diego Workforce Partnership Inc. and is currently its Vice President & Chief Operating Officer responsible for internal operations and all youth programs and he supervises the management services division. He is also on the Executive Advisory Board of Kaplan College.

William Paden

Retired educator and coach William Paden has worked in the Los Angeles Unified School District since the mid-1980s. He got his teaching credential at SDSU in 1983. William was responsible for leading championship sports teams and starting several innovative programs in the district, including the Academic Olympics. In 1996 he was the branch NAACP's Teacher of the Year, and in 2007 he was featured on the Oprah Winfrey Show and was a presenter at the Essence Festival in New Orleans.

Vincent Edward Mudd

2011 Chairman of the Board of Directors of the San Diego Chamber of Commerce (SDCC), Vincent Mudd, an SDSU business graduate (Class of '83), became a well-publicized success story when he was President and CEO of San Diego Office Interiors, winning the "Most Admired Dealership Award" in 2003 from the Workplace Alliance and in 2002 a finalist for Ernst & Young's Entrepreneur of the Year Award. He recently told his SDCC members: "As your new Chairman, I will do my best to put the 'Commerce' back in the Chamber of Commerce." Part of his plan entailed a newly created political action committee (or PAC) to realize the organization's goals. By 2012 he was on the San Diego County Water Authority representing the area on the board of the Metropolitan Water District of Southern California. In 2014, Vincent Mudd joined the architectural, interior design, and strategy communications firms Carrier Johnson + Culture as Principal and Chief Operating Officer; and he elected president of the 2014 National University Holiday Bowl and San Diego County Credit Union Poinsettia Bowl by the games' board of directors.

Dale E. Turner

Reared in San Diego, Dale Turner was awarded his certificate in materials management in 1984 then moved to Los Angeles where he found his way into acting. Since 1986 he has appeared in several movies and numerous TV series, among them "House M.D.," "ER," "Desperate Housewives," Will & Grace," "Hill Street Blues," and "Malcolm in the Middle."

Mark A. George

Upon finishing his tour of duty in the U.S. Navy, Mark A. George attended SDSU in the early 1980s before becoming a San Diego fireman and eventually rose to Deputy Fire Marshall. He has coordinated such events as the National Republican Convention, baseball World Series games, and two Super Bowls. Baptized a Mormon in 2005, he is the second counselor in the elders quorum of the Otay Mesa Ward in Chula Vista California Stake.

Donna Williams

Donna Williams Her unfortunate death at the hands of her mentally unbalanced son in July 2011 does not diminish the accomplishments of 52-year-old San Diego police detective Donna Williams who majored in social welfare at SDSU (Class of '85). The SDPD Southeast Division Officer of the Year commenced work in the Child Abuse Unit in 1989 and was popularly known as its "queen mother." Donna distinguished herself in 2002 in the nationally publicized case Danielle van Dam murder case and received an in-house citation of merit for her investigative work.

Richard Lawrence, Jr.

Richard Lawrence Jr. In 2010, Dr. Richard Lawrence, who confesses to be in his 30s, became the principal of Temecula Valley High School which has 550 students enrolled and a staff of 20. He recalls growing up in "a rough area of San Diego" but was able to get his bachelor's at SDSU (Class of '81) and doctorate at UC-San Diego/Cal State-San Marcos in 2011.

Timothy Duane Shaw

Member and chairman of the board of the Lemon Grove Elementary School District is Timothy Shaw, first appointed in 2002, elected in 2006, and reelected in 2010. Shaw has taught elementary and middle school and is a counselor at Crawford High School. He earned both his bachelor's ('83) and master's ('93) degrees at SDSU. He is also on the advisory boards of Helix Charter High School and EOP at SDSU.

Darryle J. Grimes

Darryle J. Grimes At the University of Southern California, Col. Darryle J. Grimes was a distinguished AFROTC cadet who majored in electrical engineering. He started his career as a professional soldier in 1986 and has had group and squadron commands in pilot training (he has logged more than 3,400 flight hours, 238 of which assisted missions in Iraq and the Horn of Africa), combat and special operations, and several Air Force staff positions pertaining to training and rescue operations. Leaving the Pentagon in 2012 as senior military assistant to the Assistant Secretary of the Air Force, Manpower and Reserve Affairs, he took command of the AFROTC program at SDSU (Detachment 75) which trains young officers for active duty. Grimes also has graduate degrees in aeronautical science and joint campaign planning. Among his recognitions are the Legion of Merit, Bronze Star, Kuwait Liberation Medal, Iraq Campaign Ribbon, Southwest Asia Service Medal, and the Air Medal with two oak leaf clusters.

Kevin L. Alston

Actor, comedian, journalist, reporter, Navy veteran, former Tokyo talk show host (he's fluent in Japanese) all describe SDSU graduate Kevin L. Alston, presently a business professor at San Diego Miramar College. Professor Alston has an MBA from the University of Phoenix and a doctorate from Walden University.

Rodney Mott

Rodney Mott Since 1998 Rodney Mott (Class of '86) has been a referee in the National Basketball Association (NBA). In 2013 he officiated the NBA All-Star Game. He started his career officiating San Diego high school games. Thus far he has worked nearly a thousand pro basketball games. According to one website that tracks referees, in he enjoys restoring vintage cars and charging technical fouls. A native of New Albany, Indiana, he resides in Las Vegas, Nevada.

Max Hunter

Max Hunter Having barely survived selling and ingesting illegal drugs on the meanest streets of San Diego, Max Hunter (born Derick Walter) was eventually saved by religion and academics. After two years of study at SDSU in the early 1980s he went on to get a B.A. and Ph.D. at the University of Washington and an M.A. at Harvard. Today he is Assistant Professor of Biology and Director for the Pre-Professional Health Sciences Program at Seattle Pacific University. His book is titled *Reading While Black: Reflecting on Ambivalence in Black Male Literacy Narratives in the Age of Hip Hop* (Panopticon Books, 2015).

Deidra Hardson

The Principal at Jonas Salk Elementary School in Mira Mesa, which opened in 2015, is Deidra Hardson (who had previously headed nearby Mason Elementary School from 2007 to 2014 and E. B. Scripps Elementary School from 2004 to 2007). In 1983 she was granted her bachelor's degree at SDSU and returned later to get her master's degree here.

Keith Houlemard

From Pasadena, California, Keith Houlemard played on he Aztec baseball team and graduated with business degree in 1987. After selling shoe at Nordstrom he persisted until he was hired at Nike. He worked his way up from warehouse manager, to field representative and more until 2008 he was made President the company's Jordan Brand. As the company's VP/GM of the Olympics was at the 2106 games in Rio de Janeiro. His many community involvements has garnered honors and awards.

1980'S PROFILES

Angela Cranon

The publisher of *Hollywood Scriptwriter Magazine* is Angela Cranon, an SDSU journalism graduate (Class of '83) who also has a master's degree in political science from Long Beach State. For fifteen years she was a reporter, show host, news anchor, and news director at ABC/Texas, Continental Cablevision, and the Financial News Network. She has also taught college classes public speaking, marketing and public relation, English, etc.

Carmon J. Davis

Carmon J. Davis (Class of '80) graduated from the Harvard Medical School in 1989. Earlier, she had worked as a nurse and after obtaining her M.D. at Harvard she earned an M.P.H. there, an M.S. at Yale University, and an M.B.A. at Boston College. Currently specializing in pediatrics and adolescent medicine at Boston Children's Hospital, she has published *Pediatric Emergency Care*. She is also a former director of the Harvard University Alumni Association.

Sherma Reavis-Dailey

Sherma Reavis-Dailey It has been more than thirty years since Sherma Reavis-Dailey got her bachelor's degree here in early childhood development and she has worked in the field most recently as Director of the Sunshine House Child Care Center in Marietta, Georgia.

Jeff Littlefield

The Deputy Airport Director at the San Francisco International Airport, the executive responsible for operations and security, is Jeff Littlefield, who after graduating from SDSU spent 2 years working at TWA, 2 years with America West, 21 years with United Airlines, and since 2008 has been employed at SFX. When not at work or vacationing in the Caribbean and the South Pacific he enjoys sports events and supports teen-at-risk youth organizations.

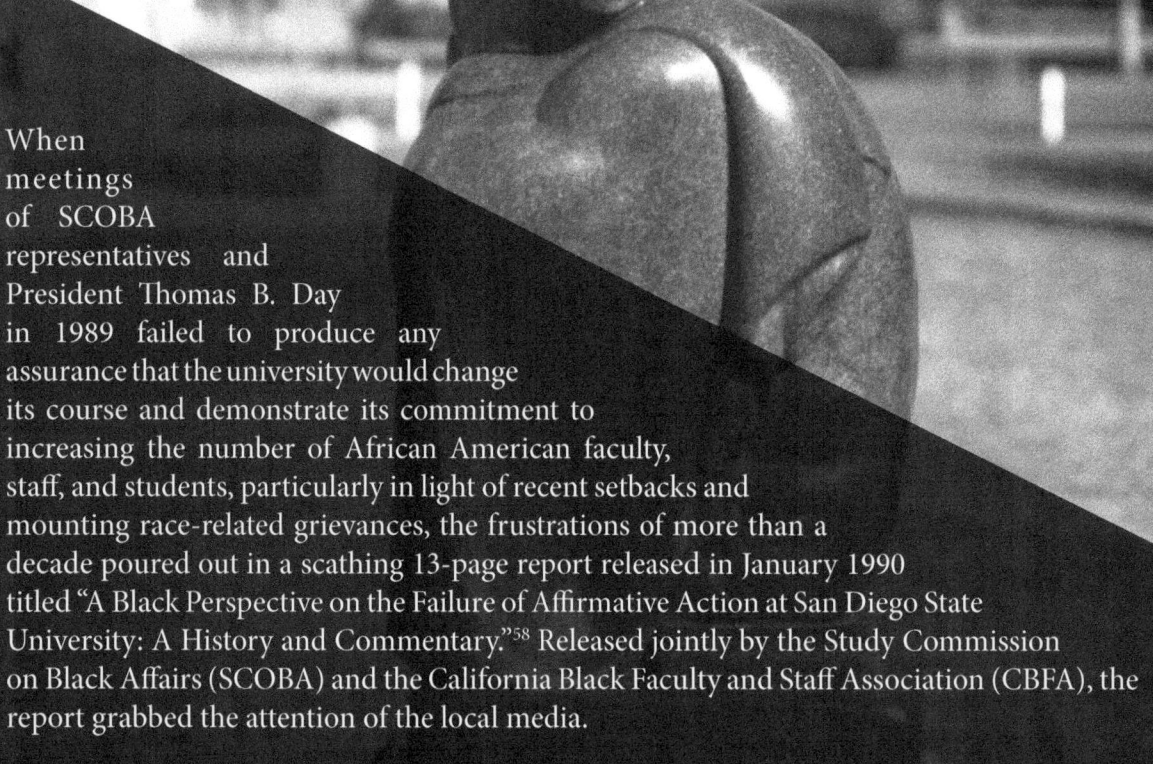

When meetings of SCOBA representatives and President Thomas B. Day in 1989 failed to produce any assurance that the university would change its course and demonstrate its commitment to increasing the number of African American faculty, staff, and students, particularly in light of recent setbacks and mounting race-related grievances, the frustrations of more than a decade poured out in a scathing 13-page report released in January 1990 titled "A Black Perspective on the Failure of Affirmative Action at San Diego State University: A History and Commentary."[58] Released jointly by the Study Commission on Black Affairs (SCOBA) and the California Black Faculty and Staff Association (CBFA), the report grabbed the attention of the local media.

A press conference was held on February 2, 1990 at which the report's primary author, Robert Fikes Jr., and other members of SCOBA and CBFSA were questioned. SCOBA co-chair Gwendolyn Patrick-Buie (then known as Gwen Hooker) told the press corps: "We truly regret the sequence of events that pushed us to go public with our experiences on this campus."[59] SCOBA co-chair E. Percil Stanford said the hard-hitting report would focus more attention on affirmative action on campus. Interviewed shortly after the press conference, political science professor E. Walter Miles reemphasized to a *San Diego Union-Tribune* reporter that there was "no encouragement given those who actively pursue black candidates for campus positions"[60]; and Prof. Shirley Weber was quoted as saying the Administration was "totally reactive and not at all

1990'S

proactive" in increasing black representation.[61] Endorsements for the report came from the faculty union (CFA); a KGTV Channel 10 television on-air editorial by its station manager; a black student solidarity rally in favor of the report held on February 16; and editorials in *The Daily Aztec* and the *San Diego Voice & Viewpoint*.

Realizing the gravity of the report which was leaked to the press prior to the press conference, President Day hastily arranged for a rare press conference of his own just minutes after the SCOBA press conference ended. This gave him an opportunity to defend his Administration's record on affirmative action, but Prof. Miles characterized Day's statement to the press as a continuation of misleading propaganda. Charges and countercharges followed late into the spring semester when a new controversy broke: the layoff of popular KPBS-TV personality Anasa Briggs-Graves (photo right) and a Hispanic producer at the station located on campus.

Over the course of a year no improvement in the status of blacks on campus was observed and this occasioned a second SCOBA/CBFSA report in 1991, "A Black Perspective on the Status of Affirmative Action at San Diego State University."[62] This 34-page update reinforced conclusions made in the first report and stressed that SDSU's record was considerably worse than other large urban campuses in the California State University system. Recommendations were offered to assist the Administration in improving its affirmative action program. As if to underscore blacks' complaints of an often abrasive, mean-spirited Administration, in late 1991 President Day effectively killed a drive that had been gaining momentum to have at least one building on campus named in honor of a African American hero. But by 1992 forces had been set in motion that would have the majority white faculty and students up in arms. President Day's plans to fire tenured professors and cut programs brought the national media to SDSU. The ensuing uprising undoubtedly forced his earlier than expected retirement.

There were other events of significance to blacks in the 1990s aside from controversies surrounding President Day and affirmative action. In 1991, alumnus Wayman Johnson's idea to have a gathering to celebrate the black presence at SDSU led to the formation of an association of black alumni which is still an active group. In 1992, the Afro-American Studies department was renamed the Department of Africana Studies, recognizing the spread of African peoples and cultures worldwide. In 1996, EOP counselor Charles Neal, along with colleague Wanda Clay Majors and Prof. JoAnne Cornwell, launched the African American Faculty/Staff Scholarship Fund, the success of which was assured thanks in part to the ingenious money raising procedure of payroll deduction. Two black students, Journard Collins and Dwayne Crenshaw, were elected back-to-back student body presidents in 1991 and 1992. Frustrated by failed attempts to have a campus building named for a distinguished African American, on May 8, 1992 members of SCOBA held a press conference at which the group symbolically renamed the Student Services Building "Bethune Hall," in honor of the famed black educator Mary McLeod Bethune. Annual Martin Luther King Jr. Day celebrations were an inspiration to many. But more than anything else, the departure of the confrontational past administration of Thomas Day and the beginning of the new, more democratic and sensitive administration of President Stephen Weber in 1997 was the long-hoped-for breath of fresh air and cause for optimism everyone could appreciate.

Cupcake LyVatt Brown: Not Your Typical Success Story

One of the most inspiring and amazing stories of triumph over personal tragedy you will ever hear is that told by Cupcake Brown (Class of `98). She got her unusual surname from hospital nurses who assumed her sedated mother was naming her baby instead of pleading for the pastry she was craving. At a young age, Brown found her mother dead from a seizure and her father and stepfather let her slip into foster care. Though she had dropped out of high school in the 10th grade, by 1987 she had a job as a legal secretary but by then was an out of control drug addict, the kind they call a "trash can junkie" who consumed every illegal substance she could get her hands on. At one point Brown wound up on the mean streets of South Central Los Angeles hustling as a prostitute. Also a gangbanger, she was shot twice, once with a 22.-caliber pistol and once with a sawed-off shotgun, and left for dead. Thanks to local attorney Kenneth Rose, Brown was able to turn her life around after hitting rock bottom. She enrolled at San Diego City College, graduated from SDSU magnum cum laude, and in 2001 finished at the top of her class at the University of San Francisco School of Law. Having worked as an attorney with Bingham McCutchen in San Francisco, Brown gives motivational speeches to youth. The title of her autobiography is *A Piece of Cake* (Crown, 2006). Some people have a hard time separating her past life with her current success. She told a reporter: "A lot of times, they're ok with me until they find out who I used to be. You know, Cupcake, she's so nice, she's so funny, then they find out, she used to be a crackhead and they grab their purse. She used to be a prostitute, they grab their husband. They begin to see me for who I was and they forget, you know."[63] She was the keynote speaker for SDSU's 2003 public administration and urban studies graduates.

Michaelanthony Brown-Cheatham: A Man On a Mission

Like a shooting star that rises and lights the heavens but quickly descends and vanishes, the young Dr. Michaelanthony Brown-Cheatham in the short time he was here far exceeded expectations in publishing articles, winning a $30,000 Ford Foundation/National Research Council grant; becoming a certified HIV trainer; and nearly completing requirements for the M.P.H degree in epidemiology/biostatistics from the SDSU-UCSD graduate school of public health. He must have realized his time on earth was very limited when he contracted the AIDS virus as he worked feverishly to inform people of the plight of young black males and to influence as many students, teachers, and children as possible. Hardly anyone was aware that Brown-Cheatham was ill. They only knew that he was a brilliant, compassionate, focused man who wanted to change things for the better in regards to African American youth. Having earned his doctorate in clinical psychology at the City University of New York, he was recruited by SDSU in 1991 and was converted from part-time to tenure track status a year later. He died from AIDS in 1995 at age 34. The University established

1990'S PROFILES

a memorial scholarship fund to extend his commitment to assist black males in their pursuit of education. A memorial paver honoring his memory is situated on the northwest side of the glass-domed University Library.

Marshall Faulk: Running for Daylight

SDSU's most publicized athlete of the decade was Marshall William Faulk. A public administration major, he selected SDSU to play football because other college teams did not want him to play at the running back position. Faulk rushed for record 4,589 yards (a school record); was a three-time All-American; and was in competition for the Heisman Trophy before leaving for the NFL his junior year. Drafted by the Indianapolis Colts in 1994, he was the league's Rookie of the Year. Faulk was traded to the St. Louis Rams in 1999. In 2002, he renewed his contract with the Rams for $44 million over 7 years—pretty good for a kid who grew up in a rough housing project in New Orleans. Faulk has established his own foundation to assist inner-city youth in areas of sports development and family life. He retired from pro football in March 2007. Known for having donated more than $1 million to charities that targeted the underprivileged in the inner cities where he played, in 2010 he was appointed to the Campanile Foundation, the philanthropic auxiliary of SDSU. On August 6, 2011 he was inducted into the Pro Football Hall of Fame.

George Benjamin Brooks, Jr.: Scientist, Executive, Publisher

After receiving a master's degree in biology at SDSU, George Brooks (Class of '90), the son of a prominent minister in Phoenix, Arizona, took his Ph.D. in aquaculture at the University of Arizona. He is Vice President for Research and Development at Rightrac Inc. in Phoenix. While in San Diego, Brooks was on the board of directors of the Elementary Institute of Science, a member of Kappa Alpha Psi Fraternity and Sigma Xi Scientific Honor Society. He was a member of the Central Arizona Water Conservation Board of Directors; a charter member and on the board of directors of Arizona Council of Black Engineers and Scientists; and a past president of the National Council of Black Engineers and Scientists. Brooks has conducted scientific studies and published scholarly papers on riparian/wetland restoration, aquaculture system design, and fish hatchery techniques. He and his wife published the online magazines *Ebony Cactus* and *NxT Horizon*.

John Arthur and John Allen Threadgill: The High Flying Twins

After graduation, airline Captains John Arthur and John Allen Threadgill (both Class of '90) received their commercial pilots licenses at Sierra Academy at Oakland International Airport and taught there for two years as flight instructors. Having flown around the globe, they credit the Black Pilots Association for giving them guidance they sometimes needed. They too have made an effort to encourage African American youth to consider careers in the airline industry. The Threadgill twins completed their probationary year with American Airlines in 1999 and were expecting to be upgraded as First Officers shortly thereafter. At that time they were based in Miami flying to points in Mexico, Central America, the Caribbean, and northern parts of South America. Today John Allen is a pilot, flight engineer and ground instructor residing in San Francisco, and John Arthur works as a pilot for American Airlines.

Carlos "Cubena" Guillermo Wilson

Born in Panama, Dr. Wilson took his doctorate at UCLA. He is an internationally respected novelist and poet. One of his works is *Orixá Changõ's Mosquitos: Short Stories and Poems* (2000), also available on CD. Wilson has chaired and taught in the Spanish & Portuguese department at SDSU since 1992. In recognition of his international renown, in 2002 he was awarded the Condecoración Nacional de la Orden Vasco Núñez de Balboa, en el Grado de Caballero by the President of Panama, Excelentísima Señora Mireya Moscoso, at a special ceremony in the Presidential Palace. He retired in 2006.

OTHER 1990'S NOTABLES

Shawn Alexander Ginwright

As a student at SDSU Shawn Ginwright (Class of '89, '92) was very active in community youth projects; and in Oakland, California he was executive director of Camp Akili which annually trained dozens of inner-city kids in the basics of self-esteem, pride, and leadership. His Ph.D. dissertation at UC Berkeley on Oakland public schools was written in 1999. Ginwright briefly taught at SDSU, San Jose State University, and Santa Clara University before he became Associate Professor of Black Studies at San Francisco State University. His book is *Black Youth Rising: Activism and Radical Healing in Urban America* (2009).

Lawrence Joseph Alfred

Assistant Dean for Underrepresented Student Programs in the College of Sciences and Professor of Biology, Dr. Alfred arrived in 1994 and was semi-retired by 2000. In addition to his scientific studies he published articles on the status of minorities in the sciences.

Matti Fountain Dobbs

From 1990 to 1999, Dr. Matti Dobbs was a full-time faculty member teaching public administration at SDSU. Since retirement she has devoted more of her time to her business enterprise called Soaring Life & Executive Coaching, a "career coaching" operation located in Carlsbad.

Bart Cameron

A political science/sociology major, Bart Cameron was the first black general manager of the campus radio station (KCR) in charge of a volunteer staff of 50 students broadcasting to an audience of 10,000.

W. Harold Tuck

As Deputy Chief Administrative Officer for the County of San Diego, W. Harold Tuck (Class of '99) is responsible for coordinating the county's law enforcement and criminal justice programs. He oversees 8,000 employees and a budget of over $1 billion. Tuck received his master's degree in public health at SDSU. In 2008 he was appointed Chief Information officer for County of San Diego. He served on the following boards of Neighborhood House Association, and Rest Haven Children's Health Fund.

Patricia Ann Wilson

Professor of Public Administration at SDSU, Dr. Patricia Wilson has published in the top journals in her discipline since her arrival in 1990. She chaired the Leonard White Award, presented by the American Political Science Association, which is given to the author of the best dissertation of the year in Public Administration. She retired in 2006 and moved to Atlanta.

Claire Forrest

Possibly the oldest person ever to have graduated from SDSU was Claire Forrest (Class of '96). A former beautician in Panama where she was born, she became a U.S. citizen in 1950 and worked as a recreational therapist and seamstress. Forrest was 85 years old when she graduated. She died at age 90 on October 7, 2001.

Charles Phillip Toombs

Since 1991 Dr. Charles Toombs (Ph.D. in English at Purdue) has taught in the Africana Studies department. He has lectured as far away as Gorlovka, Ukraine. His expertise is in African American literature and he has served as advisory editor for publications and as a referee for scholarly journals. He has published essays, book chapters, and reviews and is working on a book manuscript. A former member of the university senate's Executive Committee, in early 2010 he became California Faculty Association (CFA) chapter president and concurrently president of the campus chapter of the American Association of University Professors (AAUP).

Renee Swindle

A creative writing graduate and instructor, Renee Swindle (Class of '98) is working on her second novel. Her first try, *Please Please Please*, published by Dial/Dell in 1999, began as her M.F.A. project and became a 305-page novel that spent four months on the Blackboard Bestsellers List; was a featured selection of The Literary Guild; published in Germany as *Mehr Mehr Mehr* by Malik Press; and excerpted in *Essence* magazine. Her other novels are *Take Down the Stars* (2013), and *A Pinch of Ooh La La* (2014), both published by NAL Trade. She lives in Oakland.

James A. Raye III

A wide receiver on the Aztec football team, Jimmy Raye (Class of `91) played briefly for the Los Angeles Rams and was a high school assistant coach before working his way up in 1999 to Director of College Scouting for the San Diego Chargers. Since 2008 he has been the Chargers Director of Player Personnel.

Lloyd Francis

Owner of the Francis Tang Soo Do Martial Arts Studio, Mr. Francis taught yoga and Korean martial arts at SDSU in 1993 and he has given demonstrations of his proficiency on campus since the early 1970s.

Marlon Farley

A biology major, Dr. Marlon Farley (Class of `91) took his medical degree at UCLA and practiced family medicine in both Northern and Southern California.

Lorrie Jordan

In Charleston, South Carolina, Lorrie Jordan (Class of '96) was the WCBD-TV Channel 2 reporter and weekend weather anchor. Before she came to this NBC affiliate, Jordan worked for local San Diego station KNSD-TV as an intern then on to Texas and Los Angeles where she spent four years working on the nationwide hit show "Access Hollywood." She returned to San Diego in 2004 to work as a weathercaster for KNSD.

Victoria A. Love

A biology major, Victoria Love (Class of '99) was selected a McNair Scholar to pursue graduate study leading to the Ph.D. in immunology at Harvard University. In 2006 she completed her dissertation at Harvard, titled "Cytotoxic T Lymphocyte Antigen-4 Regulates Cytotoxic T Cells that Cause Myocarditis. She worked in vascular research, Department of Pathology, Brigham & Women's Hospital, Harvard Medical School and currently is Senior Scientist at Pfitzer Inc. in New York City working in cancer biology.

Brenda J. Means

An attorney in Everett, Washington, Means (Class of `90), Means specializes in family, real estate, landlord/tenant, and Native American and tribal law. An Africana studies major at SDSU, she got her law degree at St. Louis University.

Laura A. Harris

Dr. Laura Harris (Class of '90) is Professor of English, World Literature, and Africana Studies at Pitzer College. She took her B.A. at SDSU and her M.A. and Ph.D. in American literature at UC San Diego.

Margie N. Spikes

EOPS/CARE coordinator at San Diego City College, Margie Spikes (Class of '90) got her master's degree in counseling at SDSU.

Jarita Charmain Holbrook

With an M.S. degree in astronomy, Jarita Holbrook (Class of '92) traveled to UC Santa Cruz where she earned a Ph.D. in astronomy and astrophysics in 1997. She is only the sixth black woman to have earned a terminal degree in this field. Holbrook has taught and done research at UCLA and, presently, is an assistant research scientist at the University of Arizona. She is the principal editor of the 260-page *African Cultural Astronomy: Current Archaeastronomy and Ethnoastronomy Research in Africa* (Springer, 2008). She is the first African American to be elected chair of the historical astronomy division of the American Astronomical Society.

1990'S PROFILES

Edgar R. Hodge

Manager of Computing Systems for UC San Diego Electrical Computing and Engineering department, Edgar Hodge (Class of '91) has taught various classes on computer systems and operations at UCSD.

Shouna Shoemake

In 1994, theater major Shouna Shoemake, a soprano, won first place and $1,300 in a regional contest sponsored by New York City's Metropolitan Opera. In 2010 she was listed as a soprano in the San Diego Opera and worked as customer services representative for the Old Globe Theater.

Marvin E. Mizell

From 2011 to 2012 Marvin E. Mizell (Class of '91) was President of the 10,000-member San Diego County Bar Association. A former president of the Earl B. Gilliam Bar Association, Atty. Mizell has a B.A. from SDSU and a J.D. from UC-Davis. A San Diego native who finished Morse High School, he is a deputy attorney general in the California Attorney General's Office.

Angela Michelle Byars-Winston

Associate Professor, general internal medicine, at the University of Wisconsin –Madison School of Medicine and Public Health, Dr. Angela Byars (Classes of '91 and '92), also a graduate of Crawford High, received her bachelor's degrees in psychology and Spanish at SDSU and her Ph.D. from Arizona State University. In 2011 she was invited to the White House by President Obama to be honored as one of twelve "Champions of Change" encouraging women to choose careers in science, technology, engineering and mathematics.

Francine Foster Williams

After working as an administrator in San Diego public schools, Dr. Williams (Ph.D. SDSU/Claremont, Class of '91) became principal of Cleveland Elementary School in Pasadena, California.

Omo Awo Jahsun Olufemi Ifokolade Edmonds

Mr. Edmonds enrolled in M.F.A. classes at SDSU studying poetry. The founder of The NOMMO Collective of San Diego and the WRITERZBLOCK workshop, he has published a book of poetry titled CATABASIS; published poems in periodicals; and read his work and performed with popular artists across the country. He also taught at the Los Angeles Film School and is an African martial arts and capoeira instructor.

Marc Carter

From 1993 to 1995 Marc Carter was an outstanding forward on the Aztec basketball team. He played professionally overseas in France, Brazil, and China and back in the U.S. in the Continental Basketball League. In 1999, Carter signed to play for the Harlem Globetrotters and entertained crowds across the nation. (Another Aztec who played abroad in the 1990s and became a Harlem Globetrotter was Shawn Jamison).

Stephanie Johnson

An Africana Studies major, Stephanie Johnson (Class of '97) was awarded her law degree at Thomas Jefferson School of Law where she was president of the school's Black Law Students Association.

Kelton L. Clark

A biologist whose expertise is marine estuarine and environmental science, Dr. Kelton Clark (Class of '92) obtained his B.S. at SDSU and Ph.D. at the University of Maryland. Kelton (photo right, underwater) is a lecturer at Morgan State University and has published scientific papers. Kelton is the founder of the Society of African-American Marine Environmental Scientists.

Desiree Anastacia Byrd

Graduating with a major in psychology and a minor in Africana Studies, Desiree Byrd (Class of '94) emerged from the SDSU/UC San Diego joint doctoral program with a Ph.D. in clinical psychology in 2001. Today she is Assistant Professor of Neurology and Pathology at Mt. Sinai Medical Center in New York City.

1990'S PROFILES

Linda Morris Williams

When the chancellor of UC-San Diego was catapulted to the presidency of the University of California in 2003, he took with him Dr. Linda M. Williams (Class of '95) who had been his chief of staff (assistant chancellor). Later, Williams was Associate President of the UC system headquartered in Oakland, then in 2008 she was appointed Associate Chancellor of UC-Berkeley. She has been honored by 100 Black Men of the Bay Area for her work with youth and black students at UC-Berkeley for her mentoring and community contributions. A business major while at SDSU, she is the parent of three grown children and enjoys reading African American writers like Toni Morrison in her spare time. In 2013 she was the first recipient of the Roy Thomas Mentoring Award presented by the Department of African American Studies at UC-Berkeley and other contributions to the school's black community.

Kerry Lynne Hogan-Bean

After earning her B.A. degree in music and voice, Hogan-Bean (Class of '95), a Sigma Alpha Iota scholarship winner, went on to become Associate Director of Administration of the San Diego Opera and, later, Human Resources Manager at the Old Globe. She was a member of the Board of Directors of the San Diego Performing Arts League and the Board of Directors of the San Diego Chapter of the American Diabetes Association. She died on November 10, 2003 in Cabo San Lucas, Mexico.

Juanita Graciela McLean Cole

Having two siblings and her mother to complete degrees at SDSU, and with a strong sense of divine guidance, Juanita M. Cole (Class of '93) acquired a doctorate in developmental psychology at Howard University in 2000. She has been a post-doctoral researcher at the University of California at San Diego and a part-time instructor at SDSU. Currently, she is Associate Professor of Psychology at Azusa Pacific University.

Chanda Nicole Holsey

Dr. Chanda Holsey (Class of '93) majored in psychology at SDSU. She received the doctorate in public health at the University of Alabama in Birmingham in 2005. As director of Pediatric Asthma Programs for the American Lung Association, Southeast region, in 2004 she was the recipient of the Matthew Lee Girvin Award from the Rollin School of

Public Health at Emory University in Atlanta, Georgia for "selfless dedication to the field of public health" and for making "significant contributions toward improving the lives and health of others." In 2011 she was President-elect of the Association of Asthma Educators. Since 2008 she has been an adjunct professor of public health at SDSU. She served on the faculty of several universities, including SDSU, University of Phoenix, Nova Southeastern University, and the University of Liverpool. Inspired by her daughter, Savannah, and husband, a Navy petty officer, she authored the children's book *Savvie Sunshine, Will You Remember Daddy When I Am Out to Sea?: A Salute to All Navy Dads*.

LaShanda R. Jones-Corneille

At SDSU, LaShanda Jones (Class of '98) was a McNair Scholar who garnered the Vice Presidential Student Service Award. She later earned M.S. and Ph.D. degrees in counseling psychology at Virginia Commonwealth University. Dr. Jones teaches and is a clinician inn the Department of Psychiatry at the University of Pennsylvania School of Medicine. She has published several research papers.

Samuel Terrence Waters

In 2001 Dr. Samuel Waters (Class of '92), a former biology major at SDSU, was granted the Ph.D. in immunology at the University of Virginia. As Assistant Professor of Biological Sciences at the University of Missouri at Columbia he has done research on "a class of homeobox genes, known as the Gbx genes, which encodes DNA-binding transcription factors expressed in the developing CNS (Central Nervous System)." He has worked as a postdoctoral fellowship in the Cancer and Developmental Biology Laboratory at the National Cancer Institute.

LaVerne Seales Saley

Canisius College Spanish professor Dr. LaVerne S. Saley was born in Panama City, Panama. At SDSU she studied Latin American literature to earn her graduate degree in Spanish in 1993. She pursued the doctorate at the State University of New York at Buffalo. The daughter of school teachers, she is also fluent in French, Italian, and Portuguese. Her academic focus is Afro-Caribbean and indigenous literature and she has traveled to many foreign countries.

Myrtice Tyler

Award-winning teacher and administrator Myrtice Tyler earned both her B.A. and M.A degrees at SDSU and became AVID Coordinator for East County Schools. She taught English and reading at Monte Vista High School for eight years and was named Teacher of the Year there. She has also been the recipient of the Golden Apple Award and the Carlston Family Foundation's Outstanding Teacher's of America Award.

Grace Hawkins

Presently a retired Pennsylvania school teacher, Grace Hawkins attended SDSU in 1990 in conjunction with a program sponsored by the American Institute of Physics to train physics instructors. She earned a master's degree and later taught at Edinboro University. Ms. Hawkins also served for 15 years as a trustee for Butler County Community College and currently is on the Council of Trustees of Slippery Rock University.

Tony Clark

From Newton, Kansas, Tony Clark graduated from Christian High School in El Cajon before attending the University of Arizona on a basketball scholarship, then transferred to SDSU. A back injury led him to drop basketball and play only baseball. He was drafted by the Detroit Lions and later played for the Boston Red Sox, New York Mets, New York Yankees, Arizona Diamondbacks, and in 2008 signed on with the San Diego Padres. In 2011 he was an MLB Network studio analyst. Currently executive director of the Major League Baseball Players Association.

Ronda S. Henry-Tillman

An associate professor in the Department of Surgery at the University of Arkansas for Medical Sciences specializing in breast cancer surgery, Dr. Ronda S. Henry-Tillman is also the medical director of the UAMS's Women's Oncology Clinic and director of Cancer Control at the Arkansas Cancer Research Center. She received her B.S. in biology at SDSU and her M.D. at UC-San Diego. Dr. Henry-Tillman has published in the *American Journal of Surgery*, *Annals of Surgery*, *Journal of Breast Disease*, and *Women's Oncology Review*.

Theodosia Ballard

After 14 years of experience teaching in the city, Theodosia Ballard, who grew up in San Diego believing she would probably fail to get a college education, was named 2008-2009 Teacher of the Year, an honor awarded by the San Diego Unified School District for her outstanding accomplishments at Walter J. Porter Elementary School. Recognized for her work in mentoring colleagues and giving extra time and personal funds for her students, she continues to live in the school's vicinity. A 1993 SDSU liberal studies graduate, she next earned a master's degree.

Tracy Leighton Simmons

Assistant Dean, Admissions, Diversity Initiatives & Financial Aid at Chapman University School of Law, Tracy L. Simmons received her law degree from Golden Gate University School of Law, and her bachelor's and master's degrees respectively in psychology and education from SDSU. Before entering the field of law she was a social worker in Northern California.

Venetta Abdellatif

In Portland, Oregon the Director of Integrated Clinical Services at the Multnomah County Heath Department is Vanetta Abdellatif who earned her master's degree in public heath at SDSU. She directs dental, medical, school-based health centers, radiology and laboratory services, WIC, etc. Born into poverty, Abdellatif, who also is chairperson of the Oregon Primary Care Association, says she tries to bring "empathy and openness" to her job.

Cynthia F. Jones

At the University of Connecticut, Dr. Cynthia F. Jones is Assistant Vice President for Student Affairs. Her bachelor's degree in liberal arts and master's degree in public administration are both from SDSU, and her doctorate in higher education is from Nova Southeastern University. Prior to arriving at UConn she was Director of Career Services at Coe College in Iowa. In addition to overseeing human resources work, strategic planning and policy development, she teaches in the Higher Education program.

1990'S PROFILES

Faith Nation

In 2007 Mrs. Faith Nation (Class of '94), a clinical nurse supervisor at AccentCare Home Heath in San Diego, was named Nurse of the Year by the San Diego Black Nurses Association. A native of Jamaica, she earned her degree in nursing at SDSU and her master's degree at the University of Phoenix.

Dwane Brown

Affiliated with KPBS since the early 1990s, Dwane Brown has also worked at National Public Radio (NPR) and in the news rooms of radio and television stations in New York and San Francisco. In 2006 he was named "Best Morning Newscaster in San Diego" by the Society of Professional Journalists and the San Diego Press Club. An alumnus of Grossmont College, SDSU, and UC-Berkeley's Haas School of Business, he is often called upon to perform as master of ceremony for events held by various community groups. Blessed with a deep but soft, mellifluous voice, Brown has narrated movie, television, and radio productions.

Allen W. Estes, III.

Representing general contractors and subcontractor in construction litigation pertaining to projects mainly in California and Washington state, Allen Estes (Class of '96, political science) took his law degree at the University of California Hastings College of Law. He was a contributing author to *Construction Law Update* (Aspen Publishing, 2005 and 2008) and has made presentations on construction law at professional seminars. In 2014 he joined the firm of Gordon & Rees's Seattle office as a partner in the Construction Practice Group.

Robert Otis "Grigg" Griffith

Before he became a football analyst for KNSD Television 7/39, for 13 years Robert Griffith played pro football on four teams (Cleveland, St. Louis, Minnesota, and Arizona) and was picked for the 2000 Pro Bowl. Recognized for his community service, he received honorable mentions for the NFL's Unsung Hero Award, was the recipient of the League's Ed Block Courage Award, and was the Minnesota Vikings Community Man of the Year. In 1998 he started the Robert Griffith Foundation which has provided college scholarships to dozens of at-risk and financially disadvantaged students in San Diego.

Nora Marcella Faine-Sykes

Dr. Nora Faine, appointed to the San Diego Foundation Board of Governors in 2002, is Vice President and Chief Medical Officer of Sharp Health Plan, responsible for overseeing quality medical care and management for the plan's 43,000 members. She has lent her time and expertise to such groups as Palava Tree Inc., Children Having Children, San Diego Black Nurses, and the San Diego HIV Consumer Council. Faine, who grew up in southeast San Diego's Valencia Park, obtained her master's degree in public health from SDSU (Class of '96) and her medical degree from Meharry Medical College in Nashville, Tennessee in 1988.

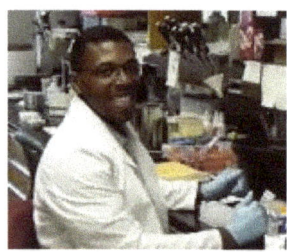

Michael Drew Davis

A chemistry major at SDSU, Dr. Davis (Class of '98, photo left) earned his doctorate in pharmacology at the University of Virginia in 2005. He works as a fellow at the National Institute of Allergy and Infectious Diseases, National Institutes of Health.

Bryan Greene

Bryan Greene is an African American artist who was born in Kentucky but was raised in England. He is a graduate of both Southwestern College and SDSU. His prints can be found for sell on the Internet, including the one on the right titled "Story Time Woman."

André José Branch

Arriving in 1999, the same year he received his doctorate at the University of Washington, Andre Branch, Associate Professor of Teacher Education, has authored scholarly articles and contributed to several books. His focused attention has been on k-12 teachers of color and ethnic identity formation in the classroom, multicultural curriculum development, and black faculty recruitment and retention. He has worked as a consultant on diversity in public education. In 2006 he trekked to rural Guatemala to establish a travel study program for SDSU students. A leader in the El Cajon Rotary, he was an active supporter of the San Diego NAACP and in 2015 he became president of this revered civil rights organization.

1990'S PROFILES

Tilisha Tionette Martin

Attorney Tilisha Martin earned a master's degree at SDSU in social work (Class of '97) and her law degree at California Western School of Law. For two years she was with San Diego County Child Welfare Services as a protective Services worker. She has worked as a dependency attorney in the county's Public Defender's Office representing minors who suffer abuse and neglect, lectured in SDSU's Social Work Graduate Program and at Cal Western, and has presented conference papers, and trained Legal Aid Society volunteers and Juvenile Hall probation officers. Currently, she is the supervising attorney for the Minors Counsel Office for Dependency Legal Group of San Diego (DLG), a nonprofit public benefit corporation.

Patricia Braswell-Burris

Class of '97 communicative disorders major Patrice Braswell-Burris also has a master's degree in deaf education and is fluent in American Sign Language. After working in the San Diego Unified School District she became a full-time faculty member at Grossmont College working in Disabled Student Services. She a member of the San Diego Deaf Advisory Committee and co-chairs the Facilities Committee at Grossmont.

P. Frank Williams

Emmy Awardwinning television producer, writer and commentator and SDSU alumnus P. Frank Williams is the founder of Profit From It Entertainment media consulting firm in Los Angeles. He has produced and written for popular television shows, among them the BET Hip Hop Music Awards (2006), the NAACP Image Awards (2005), the 2004 VIBE Awards, and the 2004 Olympics in Athens, Greece. A former editor of *The Source* magazine, he has interviewed numerous music industry stars and spoken at UC-Berkeley and USC on hip hop and popular culture. Among his TV writing/producing credits are the 2010 BET Honors on BET, 2010 BET Awards on BET, and 2009 NAACP Image Awards on FOX. Williams is founder and president of Prophet From It Entertainment, a media consulting firm with offices in Los Angeles and Toronto, assisting television, film, magazine and video game companies interface with urban audiences.

Sean Sheppard

An alumnus and former SDSU strength and conditioning coach, Sean Sheppard is the founder of the multicultural nonprofit organization called Embrace, which utilizes student volunteers and teaches underprivileged youngsters healthy lifestyles, respect for cultural differences, and feeds the homeless. Sheppard, who once was employed by the San Diego Padres as a marketing consultant, established the Sheppard Community Scholarship, administered by the SDSU's Director of Diversity, that awards $1,000 to assist qualified students in purchasing textbooks. Since 2009 he has raised nearly $40,000 to support these efforts. Said Sheppard: "I consider myself budding philanthropists. What better way to get started than by creating a fund at my alma mater that helps students learn, while providing service to a community that I care about deeply." His nonprofit organization, Embrace, has garnered awards and the attention of politicians across California for uplifting needy veterans and guiding youth toward community service.

Abdi Mohamoud

With a MBA from SDSU and a management certificate from Stanford University, Mr. Mohamoud is Executive Director of Horn of Africa, serving the city's East African community. In 2004 he was picked as one of the area's top under 40 business leaders by The San Diego Metropolitan Magazine.

Ashanti H. Hands

In 2000, Ashanti H. Hands was named Dean of Student Affairs at UC-San Diego's Thurgood Marshall College. The former SDSU graduated student in education was appointed Dean of Students at San Diego Mesa Community College in 2007 where she oversees oversees 25,000 students.

Nola Butler Byrd

Scholar-activist and alumna Nola Butler Byrd earned her master's degree at SDSU in 1999 and completed the joint doctoral program in with Claremont Graduate School in 2004. An associate professor of counseling and school psychology and director of Community-Based Block Program, she led the faculty union's effort at the university to increase black and minority hiring and retention. Off campus she has been involved with various social justice organizations, among the Planned Parenthood and the National Conference for Community and Justice.

1990'S PROFILES

Deon Taylor

Escaping the violent streets of Gary, Indiana, Dean Taylor and his mom found a better life in Sacramento. Later a biology major at SDSU (Class of '98), he played on the Aztec basketball team his four years and then briefly pro basketball in Germany where he discovered an interest in screenwriting and filmmaking. *Dead Tone* (2007), the first movie he wrote and directed, was followed by his BET television series *Nite Tales*. His slasher/thriller *Chain Letter* was released in 2010. Taylor teamed up with Oscar-winning actor Jamie Foxx to produce the fall 2011 NBC television series mobster drama *Tommy's Little Girl*. In 2014 he was set to direct the action film "Free Agent" and reportedly had two other projects in post-production.

Felix Goodson

After a decade in the student travel business specializing in spring break events and then working on projects for NASCAR, the National Hot Rod Association, and golf's U.S. Open, Felix Goodson, who last attended SDSU in 1998, joined San Diego-based VAVi Sport & Social Club as the company's vice president and chief operating officer.

Kevin B. Winkler

Upon obtaining his degree in theatre at SDSU in 1976, Kevin Winkler earned graduate degrees at Columbia University and Hunter College. A past president of the Theatre Library Association (TLA), he is Assistant Director for Access Services at the New York Public Library for the Performing Arts and Visiting Assistant Professor of Library & Information Science at Pratt Institute. Kevin has co-authored an entry on performing arts in libraries in the *International Dictionary of Library Histories* (2001).

Regina Malveaux

With a degree in social policy from SDSU (Class of '97), Regina Malveaux entered law school at Howard University. While at Howard she was a White House intern for First Lady Hillary Rodham Clinton and a Congressional intern for Maxine Waters of California when she chaired the Congressional Black Caucus. Her work on behalf of women and children has been recognized with numerous awards, including the Judge Adolfo Birch Public Service Award and being named a "40 Leaders Under 40" by San Diego Metropolitan Magazine. Regina has taught as an adjunct professor at La Sierra and San Diego State Universities. In 2013 she was named Executive Director of the Spokane, Washington YWCA.

Priese Printz Lamont Board

Grammy-nominated songwriter-producer Printz Board (born Priese Prince LaMont Board) was instrumental in launching the highly popular Hip Hop-Pop group known as The Black Eyed Peas. A music scholarship brought him Columbus, Ohio to SDSU where was a double major in music and business. By the time he was a senior in 1996 his bands Gangbusters and Phazz had performed throughout California. His big break came when he joined the Black Eyed Peas as music director and keyboard player. Printz contributed six tracks on the groups 2010 album "The E.N.D". He has collaborated with entertainment giants like Brian Setzer, Justin Timberlake, Busta Rhymes, John Legend, Katy Perry, Michael Jackson and Backstreet Boys, and has scored television movies and commercials for Victoria's Secret, Pepsi, and Benefiber. He owns the production company Beets & Produce that has a clothing line and among his businesses is a vodka brand, a restaurant, and a night club. In 2013 he launched his solo career, releasing his first single.

Kim Folsom

Kim Folsom specializes in video-based support tools for tech companies. The founder and CEO of ShowUhow Inc. and, prior to this, VP-General Manager of DriveCam and founder and CEO of SeminarSource, she has an economics degree from SDSU and an MBA from Pepperdine University. Kim has advised the Consumer Electronic Association, SDSU Entrepreneur Management Center, Sheppard Venture, Qualcomm Stadium and the San Diego Bowl Committee.

Kris Marsh

University of Maryland sociology professor Kris Marsh got her undergraduate degree at SDSU (Class of '96) and her Ph.D. at USC. At UMD-College Park she is also affiliated with the Maryland Population Research Center (she has a graduate certificate in geographic information science), Department of Women's Studies, and Department of African American Studies. Her areas of expertise are the black middle class, race and educational attainment, and intra-racial health disparities.

Brandi Wells

Licensed psychologist and certificated school psychologist Dr. Brandi Wells runs Wells Psychological and Educational Services in Kennesaw, Georgia. With a B.A. in psychology (1997) and M.S. in counseling (2001), both from SDSU, she took her doctorate at Georgia State University. A member of American Psychological

Association et al., she has presented papers at professional meetings and published her research. She has also been employed as a psychologist in The Pediatric Therapy Clinic in Kennesaw.

Edwin Olweny

A licensed professional engineer, Edwin Olweny (Class of '90), a native of Kenya, is a principal at Los Angeles-based Hopper Engineering Associates and is the Secretary of Harambee Investments, LLC, a real estate company located in Orange, California but focused on properties in Kenya. In Kenya he is director at Engineered Construction Systems Intl. Corp.

Tia Boatman-Patterson

Atty. Tia Boatman-Patterson (SDSU Class of '90) is General Counsel of the Sacramento Housing and Redevelopment Agency. Among other things, she oversees issues put before the City Council and Board of Supervisors or that impact the Redevelopment Agency and/or Housing Authority. Prior to this, the McGeorge Law School graduate was Special Assistant to the Speaker of the California Assembly and Senior Associate with Best Best & Krieger LLP in the Municipal and Redevelopment Practice group, contributing her expertise on housing authorities, public housing, urban redevelopment, and municipal law to the Sacramento firm.

La'Roi Damon Glover

San Diego native and professional football defensive tackle La'Roi Glover played for 13 years with four teams and was honored in being picked to appear in six Pro Bowls. At Point Loma High School he was a top ranked shot putter and at SDSU, where he graduated with a degrees in public administration and sociology, he was named first team All-WAC. In 2010 he was hired as Director of Player Personnel for the Saint Louis Rams. In 2012 he earned his MBA at Fontbonne University.

Shawn Martel Moore

While serving for 23 years in the U.S. Navy and Reserves, Shawn M. Moore graduated magna cum laude at SDSU with a degree in criminal justice (Class of '92) and several years later got her law degree at Syracuse University. A former Deputy Court Clerk in San Diego, she is Director of the Tompkins County (New York) Human Rights Commission, she is now Deputy County Administrator & Director Human Rights in Tompkins County

Kristen M. Howard

An attorney in the law firm of Makupson & Howard located in Pasadena, Kristen M. Howard (psychology, Class of '96) picked up her law degree at the American College of Law in Anaheim, California, and interned at the Los Angeles District Attorney's Office. She has been a volunteer for the Los Angeles County Bar Pro Bono Domestic Violence Project and the Harriett Buhai Center for Family Law. Currently, she is a partner in the firm of Makupson & Howard

Richard D. Epps

UCLA Ph.D. candidate Richard D. Epps has been a lecturer in the political science department at SDSU since 1998. He has done field research in the Middle East and North Africa and has taught courses on international relations, American politics, and comparative politics of the Third World. A faculty advisor to Greek organizations and student athletes, he designed a peer mentoring/tutoring program and has worked closely with EOP.

John P. Hamilton

Hamilton & Associates Consultants, a Los Angeles education firm owned by Dr. John P. Hamilton, specializes in bettering African American students, particularly males. A sociology major at SDSU (Class of '92), Hamilton earned his educational doctorate at the University of La Verne in 2005. Among others, he has worked for both the Compton and Los Angeles Unified School Districts. He has served on the Board of Trustees of the Compton Community College District and worked as an administrator at UCLA and Cal State-Long Beach where he has been a part-time faculty member.

John G. Lewis

A professional interpreter for two decades, John Lewis, who majored in French at SDSU (Class of '91) has provided interpreting services in American Sign Language, Spoken English, and Spoken French. He was granted his linguistics graduate degree at Gallaudet University and works as the VSR Manager at Gallaudet University Interpreting Service (GIS). John is also a founding member of the National Alliance of Black Interpreters Inc.

Maurice A. Bell

Specializing in internal medicine at St. Mary Medical Center in Long Beach, California, Dr. Maurice Bell (Class of '92) was a biology major at SDSU. He earned his MD from UC San Francisco School of Medicine.

Tiffany Thomason

Since 2006, Tiffany Thomason (Class of '99) has taught English at The Preuss School at UC-San Diego, reputed to be the top charter school in California. In earning her master's degree in education at Stanford University, Tiffany compiled a 4.0 GPA. She returned to her native San Diego after teaching in San Mateo for a while.

Pamela Lloyd-Ogoke

New York City native Pamela Lloyd-Ogoke became deaf during her adolescence but this did not deter her from achieving two college degrees. In 1990 she completed the post-M.A. deafness rehabilitation administration program at SDSU. Today she is Chief of Community Service for the North Carolina Division of Vocational Rehabilitation. She also serves on the Gallaudet University Board of Trustees and is a past president of the National Black Deaf Advocates.

Emmett G. Shaffer

Dr. Emmett Shaffer (Class of '92) is the Vice President of Business Development and Marketing for the Georgia Leadership Institute for School Improvement (GLISI). He has a master's degree in counselor education from SDSU and a doctorate in education from the University of West Georgia. Before arriving at GLISI he was a middle school principal, a school district administrator, and had worked in two Fortune 500 companies.

Estralita Mary Elizabeth Martin

Estralita Martin (Ph.D., UC-Berkeley), a developmental biologist, arrived at SDSU in 1993 to teach general biology and embryology. She was a faculty advisor to student groups before being appointed Assistant Dean for Student Affairs and Director of the Center for the Advancement of Students in Academia (CASA), both in the College of Sciences. She has been recognized for her exceptional work in planning for student diversity, counseling, retention, and successful academic outcomes.

Michael DeWitt Washington

In September 2013, Michael D. Washington, a Republican appointed by Democratic Gov. Jerry Brown, was sworn in as San Diego County Superior Court Judge. A former SDSU business major (Class of '90), he earned his J.D. degree at the California Western School of Law. From 1994 to 2013 he was a county deputy public defender. Among his recognitions are the Richard D. Westbrook Memorial Award for Outstanding Trial Advocacy and the California Western School of Law Faculty Award for Outstanding Scholarship and Service.

Yolanda Pam Gammill

Yolanda P. Gammill, a graduate of SDSU who finished the California Western School of Law and was admitted to the California Bar in 1999, has been an administrative law judge with the California Unemployment Insurance Appeals Board. She has had law offices in Del Mar and Oakland, California.

Amanda Jeremiah Thomas

Aerospace engineering graduate Amanda Thomas (Class of '97) was born in Grenada, West Indies, but at age 15 her family moved to Pasadena, California, close to NASA's Jet Propulsion Laboratory. As luck would have it, she found her way to SDSU where she was mentored by an extraordinary upperclassman who later worked at JPL and eventually she too found work with him on the Mars "Curiosity" project that successfully landed a rover that explored the surface of the "red planet." For this, along with four other SDSU alums who worked on the project, she was awarded an alumni Monty in 2013. Currently, Thomas is supervisor at NASA's Deep Space Network in the Mojave Desert.

Adam Russell Jeffers

An SDSU career counselor in Career Services, Dr. Adam R. Jeffers is an alumnus of SDSU (Class of '96) who acquired his doctorate in education at the University of Southern California in 2010. Aside from his career counseling work he has given presentations on the history of Islam in regard to African Americans and on serving the needs of Muslim students.

Dempster R. Cherry

A registered representative/investment advisor with Nelson Securities Inc., Dempster R. Cherry, an SDSU graduate and U.S. Army veteran, also writes a financial advice column for "The Chocolate City Voice," a positive and inspirational online magazine, founded by SDSU alum Gwen Price, distributed in a dozen states including California, Texas, New York, Florida, and Pennsylvania.

Dawan Percil Stanford

The son of distinguished SDSU Professor Emeritus E. Percil Stanford, Dawan P. Stanford took his undergraduate degree in business at SDSU and his law degree at UC-Berkeley. He was admitted to the California Bar in 1997. Among other firms he worked as an attorney at Morrison and Foerster, Symantec Corporation, arranging plans for new and mid-sized business enterprises and multinationals. Upon earning a doctorate at the European Graduate School in Saas Fee, Switzerland, he taught there as an associate professor and published the book Novel Imagery: Aesthetic Response as Feral Laboratory (Atropos Press, 2009), concerning new perceptions of traditional media. He founded Fluid Hive LLC, a consultancy focused on improving organizations, then co-created Folding Voice with his father to advise those working in the field of gerontological care. Currently, he is operations director at the Education Design Lab in Washington, DC.

Nelson B. Robinson

In the 1980s and 1990s Nelson Robinson was a consultant and procurement manager at the SDSU Foundation's Minority Business Development Center, but his previous career was in aviation. At age 17 he was a cadet in Civil Air Patrol, trained as an airplane mechanic in Mississippi, serviced P-47s for the Tuskegee Airmen, and in 1946 commenced his career in the newly desegregated U.S. Air Force, eventually becoming an aircraft line crew chief and retiring as a master sergeant. A licensed pilot himself, in 1991 he was elected to the International Aerospace Hall of Fame board of directors periodically accepted speaking engagements and donations to the Tuskegee Airmen Scholarship Fund.

Chemin Tate

Already the mother of her first child while an undergraduate at SDSU, Dr. Chemin Tate (Class of '99) was a fellow of the Minority Biological Research Support program (MBRS). She earned her M.D. at the University of Chicago's Pritzker School of Medicine in 2004. In private practice as an OB/Gyn for three years, she next took a faculty position at the University of Indiana School of Medicine and has lectured abroad.

In 1990, there were 1,405 African American students attending SDSU. By 2001, there were 1,374 representing 4.1 percent of the student population, but in the fall of 2009 the situation had worsened to 1,28w8 enrolled, just 3.9 percent. Even more disappointing than the stagnant growth rate of black students is the fact that between 1992 and 2000 the continuation rate for first-time black freshman dipped from 69 percent to 61.3 percent. No other ethnic group suffered such setbacks in the periods reported by the Office of Institutional Research.

The graduation rate for black Aztec athletes, as tracked annually by two independent agencies, remained one of the worse in the nation over the past decade. Save for the arrival of three black librarians and the hiring of a black vice president for Student Affairs and his black associate vice presidents, anecdotal information concerning the hiring of black faculty and staff has also not been encouraging. The protracted tenure battle of Dr. Patricia A. Washington (Women's Studies) was quite unsettling. On April 18, 2005 a California Superior Court dismissed Dr. Washington's discrimination lawsuit against the university. She had been denied tenure in 2002. In the wake of Dr. Washington's well-publicized battle to regain her position, in October 2006 EOP counselor Charles C. Neal, employed at SDSU since 1981, filed a lawsuit against university officials charging racial discrimination after he was denied promotion to associate director of EOP.

Direct testimony by black faculty and staff personnel in the fall of 2004 to members of the WASC teams accrediting criticizing the university's recent record of hiring, promotion, and tenure was

21st Century

essentially ignored and, of considerable disappointment to those who had bothered to communicate their concerns, the evidence they presented was not reflected to any degree in the team's review report issued in 2005 and 2006. On May 6, 2005 the San Diego branch of the NAACP challenged an 18-page study titled "Report on African American Faculty Diversity at SDSU," issued by a subcommittee of the Faculty Senate which was set up to examine the attrition of black faculty. Believing the subcommittee's approach to be flawed and its recommendations timid, the NAACP sent out a press release criticizing the report for failing to offer "concrete and measurable outcomes and timeframes" and for revealing "a lack of seriousness on the part of the university."

But an appropriate response to all of this was hardly possible as SCOBA and CBFSA had ceased their watchdog activities and protests years earlier when these groups, in effect, disintegrated after their well-publicized battles with the Administration in the early 1990s. And it remains to be seen if the torch is to be passed on to a new generation of black leaders on campus. For the second time in the university's history, black students were elected back-to-back presidents of the Associated Students (Ron Williams in 2001 and Priscilla Ocen in 2002) and in 2005 Chris Manigault was elected AS president. The April 2004 issue of *Ebony* magazine carried a photo of SDSU Homecoming Queen Shani Etter, then a senior business administration major from Carson, California. It was reported in 2013 that the graduation rate for black student at SDSU had increased significantly, from 28.6% in 2002 to 55.8% in 2011. In the same period the Latino graduation rate jumped from 31.4% to 58.8%.

Ron Williams   Pricilla Ocen   Chris Manigault

In an unprecedented flurry of hiring, three black librarians arrived over a four month period in 2002: Kathryn Neal (Special Collections & Archives), Jon E. Cawthorne (Administration), and Gloria L. Rhodes (Outreach). Other new century hires include Drs. Francis Njubi Nesbitt (currently chair department chairman) and Adisa A. Alkebulan in Africana Studies; Drs. Tonika D. Green, Nola B. Byrd, Frank Harris III, Lenoar Foster, Joseph Johnson, and Angela S. McIntosh in the College of Education; Dr. Kyle W. Farmbry in Public Administration; Dr. Paul Minifee in Rhetoric & Writing Studies; Dr. Kimala J. Price in Women's Studies; Dr. Kyra R. Greene in Sociology; Dr. Samuel Kassegne in Engineering, and the philosophy department converted Dr. John A. Berteaux's lecturer position to full-time tenure track. But the flurry of new faculty hires were more than offset by retirements and resignations.

Francis N. Nesbitt   Tonika D. Green   Angela McIntosh   Kyle W. Farmbry

Jon Cawthorne   Kimala J. Price   Paul Minifee

THE 21ST CENTURY

The year 2002 saw two SDSU alumni, Dwayne Crenshaw (Class of `93) and Charles L. Lewis (Class of `91) competing against each other to fill the 4th District San Diego City Council seat held by George L. Stevens (Class of `58) since 1991. Lewis won but died in office from liver complications on August 8, 2004.

D. Crenshaw

Charles Lewis

PROFILES
21ST CENTURY NOTABLES

Terry Warren Johnson

Elected as the first black mayor of Oceanside, California in 2000, Johnson, a candidate for a degree in public administration at SDSU, had previously served two terms on the City Council. A native of Oceanside, he lost reelection in 2004.

Lauralyn Electra Miles Electra Cooke

Another product of the SDSU/UCSD joint doctoral program, Dr. Lauralyn Miles completed her dissertation and was awarded the terminal degree in clinical psychology in 2002. A licensed psychologist, she works at Kaiser Permanente in South San Francisco Medical Center in the Department of Behavioral Medicine.

Helen Rochelle Kemp

In January 2002, Helen Kemp completed requirements for her Ph.D. in chemistry via the joint doctoral program of SDSU and UC San Diego. Kemp was supported by the Minority Biomedical Research Support (MBRS) program, funded by the National Institutes of Health/National Institute of General Medical Sciences. Currently, she is a research associate at Proctor & Gamble.

Richard Douglas Hector

With the intent of only getting an A.S. degree to better his chances to supervise a forklift crew, Dr. Richard Hector (Class of '01) enrolled at a junior college and discovered he was good at math and science. With a B.S. from UC San Diego and a M.S. in neuroscience from UC San Francisco, Hector pursued the master's in public health at SDSU. He was awarded a Fulbright Scholarship in 1999 to study the healthcare system in his native Trinidad and Tobago. He has published in the international journal *Quality of Life Research* and the *West Indian Journal of Medicine*. Richard studied for a doctorate in public health at UCLA and today is President/CEO of Associated Healthcare Analysts, LLC in Phoenix Arizona.

21ST CENTURY PROFILES

James R. Kitchen

Upon his arrival in 2000, Dr. James Kitchen, Vice President for Student Affairs, had to deal with two crises which received national attention: a case where a fraternity pledge nearly died of an alcohol overdose; and protests against the university's Aztec mascot. He handled both situations quite admirably. A personable and popular man, he retired in 2013.

Kyle Westly Farmbry

As a 19-year-old sophomore at George Washington University, Kyle Farmbry published a book on Southeast Asian emigrants titled *The String Bracelet: Reflections of and by the Young People of Southeast Asia*; and at age 20 wrote an editorial in the *Washington Post*. He later became president of the student body. In 2001, Dr. Farmbry was hired as Assistant Professor of Public Administration at SDSU. He left in 2004 to teach at the University of Texas at San Antonio.

Ethan Neil Kendricks

Accepted into the Kodak American Intern Pavillion Intern Program, Kendricks was a videographer at the 2003 Cannes Film Festival. A graduate student in television and film, his freelance writings have appeared in the *San Diego Union-Tribune*, *Artweek*, *The Independent Film and Video Monthly*, *MovieMaker Magazine*, and *KPBS On Air*; and his artwork and photography have graced the San Diego Art Museum and London's Royal College of Art. In 2005 he was hired as film curator of the Museum of Contemporary Art San Diego. He earned his master's degree at SDSU in 2006. He is currently an instructor in the School of Arts & Communications at Southwestern College He is also film curator for San Diego's Museum of Contemporary Art and is currently teaching a screenwriting class at SDSU. His latest documentary is "Comics Are Everywhere."

Adisa A. Alkebulan

Arriving in 2002 in the Africana Studies department, Alkebulan (Ph.D., Temple University) specializes in Pan-African languages in the Caribbean and the U.S. and also history. In 2003, he traveled to South Africa to assist in HIV/AIDS awareness and prevention. He is on the editorial board of the *Journal of Black Studies*.

John Browning

Following a national search, former Gardena, California Police Department Captain John Browning began his post as SDSU police chief on December 19, 2005. a resident of Temecula, he retired in 2013.

Johnny Eaddy

In 2007, Johnny Eaddy, Associate Director of Physical Plant, celebrated 20 years employment at SDSU. During this time he not only managed technical and personnel matters but also contributed articles to *Cleaning & Maintenance Management* and *Housekeeping*.

Darlene V. Willis

A psychologist, Dr. Willis was appointed Dean of Students in 2005, having previously served as executive administrative officer for student affairs at UC-San Diego. She graduated from Harvard University's Institute for Management and Leadership Education and co-founded Concerned Parents Alliance. She left SDSU in February 2007.

Kristian L. Brown

In 2005, while a medical school student at UC-San Diego, Dr. Brown (Class of '00) won the Thomas E. Carew Prize for Cardiovascular Research. He has published in the *American Journal of Physiology and Heart Circulation Physiology* and the *Journal of Burn Care & Research*, among others. In addition to medical doctorate he has a Ph.D. in biomedical engineering from Wayne State University, with honors. His specific discipline interest is abdominal solid organ transplant surgery. He works in the Department of General Surgery at Wayne State's School of Medicine.

Otis Lawrence Stitt III.

Upon completing his studies at SDSU in 1999, Dr. Stitt entered Meharry Medical School in Nashville, Tennessee. By 2007 he was chief resident in the Department of Ob/Gyn & Reproductive Sciences at the University of Maryland School of Medicine. In 2011 he was a physician a St. Francis Hospital in Columbus, Georgia.

Sinead Natasha Younge

Africana Studies major Sinead Younge (Class of '00) went on to obtain her Ph.D. in community psychology and urban affairs at Michigan State University in 2005. A published researcher, she currently works as Associate Professor of Psychology at Morehouse College.

Dontia Haynes

The September 2005 traffic accident that killed star tennis player Dontia Haynes, a senior who had planned to marry and start a family, shocked the university. Dontia had transferred to SDSU from UC-Irvine, made the MWC All-American team, and played in matches with Serena and Venus Williams. A member of SDSU's 2005 Mountain West Championship team, his racket and shoes were donated to the university's Hall of Fame in a ceremony a year after his death.

Andre Todd Creese

A psychology major at SDSU, Dr. Creese (Class of '90) later earned his medical degree and today is Medical Director and Chief of the Emergency Department of Florence, South Carolina's McLeod Regional Medical Center, and has been touted as a pioneer in introducing cost effective means to reduce patient deaths caused by accident and deficient service. A 2007 Monty Award recipient, he also serves as medical director for the Darlington Raceway.

Samuel Kinde Kassenge

Arriving in 2005 in the College of Engineering, Dr. Kassegne has a Ph.D. in mechanical engineering from Virginia Tech (other degrees were earned in India and Turkey). A native of Ethiopia who fled the country during the civil war of the early 1980s, he previously worked at UC-San Diego and UC-Irvine. Promoted to Associate Professor at SDSU in 2010, he is the co-founder of the American-based Ethiopian Computing and Information Technology Association.

Lori S. White

Dr. White, whose doctorate from Stanford is in education, for two years was associate vice president for student affairs and dean of students. She left SDSU in 2004 to take a similar post at the University of Southern California and Southern Methodist University.

Sahra Abdi

Winner of the 2006 California Peace Prize ($25,000), presented by the California Wellness Foundation, is Sahra Abdi (Class of '02). Herself an immigrant who arrived from Somalia a decade ago, Mrs. Abdi is employed as program coordinator at the City Heights Wellness Center, sponsored by Children's Hospital and Scripps Health, which provides counseling and training in the areas of stress management, health, education, and violence prevention to San Diego's immigrant community. She is a community organizer who formerly (2006- 2010) worked at Scripps Health.

Evette Hornsby-Minor

At SDSU Evette Hornsby-Minor was awarded her B.A. in Africana Studies, M.A. in counseling, and, in 2004, her Ph.D. in education (SDSU/Claremont). She is Assistant Professor of Gender Studies at St. Lawrence University in Canton, New York. Previously, she worked at SDSU as director of its Future Educators' Center and was a visiting faculty member at Southern Illinois University and the University of Minnesota.

Priscilla Ocen

Elected student body president in 2003, Priscilla Ocen completed a legislative fellowship in the California State Assembly and subsequently entered UCLA law school on scholarship. In June 2007 she was student speaker at the law school graduation ceremony and was selected to clerk for a federal judge in Detroit, Michigan. In 2011 she was a Critical Race Studies Law Fellow at UCLA examining the complex factors leading to the incarceration of black females. Today she is Associate Professor of Law at Loyola Marymount University.

Kassim Osgood

Avoiding the temptation to place athletics above getting a diploma, 6 ft. 5in. 220lb. Kassim Osgood (Class of '02) graduated with a degree in sociology and for the past five years has been an outstanding wide receiver and special teams player for the San Diego Chargers. Selected to play in the 2007 Pro Bowl, he has been recognized for his Team KO program for San Diego youth and other community service.

William and Marcus Demps

Will and Marcus Demps

Brothers William Demps and Marcus Demps played football at SDSU. Older brother William, an IDS major, went on to play pro football for the Baltimore Ravens, New York Giants and the Houston Texans. Marcus, a criminal justice major, played for the Detroit Lion in 2006. Both played the safety position. Because their mother is Korean, they speak the language conversationally. In 2010, Will opened "Wet Willie's," a bar/restaurant chain franchise, in San Diego's fashionable Gaslamp District.

Frank Harris III.

Lured from the University of Southern California where he obtained his doctorate, wrote an award-winning dissertation, and was Associate Director of USC's Center for Urban Education, Dr. Frank Harris III arrived at SDSU in 2007. He is Associate Professor of postsecondary education and co-director of the Minority Male Community College Collaborative (M2C3) He has published on the theme of black males in higher education.

Cheryl James-Ward

Dr. Cheryl James-Ward (Ed.D., USC) had diverse experiences in public schools throughout California (including being an elementary school principal in Long Beach, Encinitas, and Pasadena) before landing at SDSU in 2007 as Assistant Professor of Educational Leadership. She is also Director of the Chinese and American Educational Leadership Symposium. She is the primary author of the book *Using Data to Focus Instructional Improvement* (Association for Supervision & Curriculum Development, 2013

Aaron and Tanis Starck

Aaron and Tanis Starck

Dr. Tanis Starck, Director of the Office of Intercultural Relations and the Cross Cultural Center, and husband Aaron Starck, formerly Associate Director of Career Services, arrived in California along with hundreds of refugees from the devastation that befell New Orleans in 2005. Prior to the great deluge Tanis had taught psychology at Tulane University and Aaron had been director of Loyola University's Upward Bound program. Thankfully, the pair found employment at SDSU where they could rendezvous for snacks in East Commons.

Kyra Renea Greene

Kyra Renea Greene Assistant Professor of Sociology Kyra R. Greene previously worked at Stanford University (where she earned her doctorate) as a "diversity director," and taught at Rider University in New Jersey before landing at SDSU in 2007. She has co-authored a book chapter on affirmative action.

Ephriam Salaam and Chester Pitts

Ephraim Salaam & Chester Pitts Former SDSU football players Ephraim Salaam and Chester Pitts, both played for the Houston Texans pro team, made Super Bowl history when they appeared together in a 60-second commercial during the 2008 contest. The ad promoting the National Football League won the Super Ad competition which was decided by fans nationwide who logged on and cast their votes on NFL.com/superad. In 2011 Salaam was a free agent; Pitts was with the Seattle Seahawks. In 2012, Pitts started a career as a sportscaster at KPRC-News 2 in Houston, Texas, and in 2013appeared in the 23rd season of "The Amazing Race" Salaam.

Beverly Lynn Booker

An assistant professor of Counselor Education, Dr. Booker (Ph.D., University of Louisville, 2003) arrived at SDSU in 2007 having previously worked as a high school counselor in Virginia. Her research has focused on "perceptions and outcomes of collaboration of school counselors and administrators in schools to impact student achievement." She left SDSU in 2011 to teach a Cal State-Long Beach.

21ST CENTURY PROFILES

Steven C. Collins

A former president of the Southeast Rotary, Mr. Collins was also an executive committeeman assisting three area chambers of commerce; was on the board of Neighborhood House Association and the San Diego Police Citizen Review Board; and was a member of the City of San Diego Salary-Setting Commission. He had previously worked as a broadcaster in Erie, Pennsylvania and San Francisco before coming to San Diego. In the fall of 2001 he was hired as SDSU's Manager of Government and Community Relations. Just weeks before his death at age 54 on March 8, 2008, he was announced the winner of the Union Bank KPBS Black History Month Local Heroes Award.

K.D. Aubert

Born in Louisiana, Karen Denise Aubert played on the Aztec women's softball team. Discovered while working at a cosmetics counter in Macy's, she became a fashion model and appeared in commercials promoting Fanta soda, Noxzema, Victoria's Secret, Frederick's of Hollywood, Bacardi, Coca Cola, etc. To date she has appeared on three television shows ("Buffy the Vampire Slayer," "Kidnapped," and "Bones"); in seven music videos; and among her nine movie acting credits are "The Scorpion King" (2002), "Soul Plane" (2004), "The Grand" (2007), "Still Waiting" (2009) and "Turning Point" (2012)

Naomi M. Hall-Byers

After obtaining her master's degree in public health at SDSU, in 2007 Naomi Hall earned her Ph.D. in psychology at Claremont Graduate University. She is Associate Professor of Psychology at Winston-Salem State University in North Carolina.

Brandon Loyvon Heath

The top scorer in Aztec and Mountain West Conference basketball history is Brandon L. Heath who was awarded his degree in sociology. Signed by the Los Angeles Lakers in September 2008, the L.A. native was put on waivers a month later and started playing guard for the Los Angeles D-Fenders, an NBA Development League team owned by the Lakers. He played for pro teams in France, Bulgaria, and Cyprus. In 2013 he signed with the Sacramento Kings but was waived a month later and returned to play in Bulgaria.

Traci D. Howard

Assistant Dean Traci Howard heads the Admissions department at California Western School of Law in San Diego. She had previously worked there in Student Diversity Services. Howard obtained her master's in educational leadership at SDSU and has been quite active in the Law School Admissions Council.

Ticey L. Hosley

Grossmont College counselor Ticey Hosley obtained her doctorate in 2007 in higher education through the auspices of SDSU and the Claremont Graduate University. A proud alumna of Lincoln High, she has been very active in the school alumni association and has contributed substantially to political campaigns (photo left at Obama Inauguration).

Deitre Collins-Parker

In February 2009 former collegiate volleyball Olympian and former outstanding Cornell University and University of Nevada-Las Vegas head coach Deitre Collins-Parker was named to lead the Aztec's women's volleyball team. While at UNLV she was honored as the Western Athletic Association's 1988 Coach of the Year, and at Cornell seven of her player made first-team All-Ivy. A graduate of the University of Hawaii, in 2008 she was inducted into the American Volleyball Coaches Association Hall of Fame and has served on the association's board of directors. Her husband, Dale Parker, is a basketball coach.

Juel Ann Giddens Moore

With her doctorate in education (SDSU/Claremont Graduate University, 1998) Juel Moore served as principal of Oak Park Elementary School and president of the Association of African American Educators (AAAE). In 2007 she was selected by the women's auxiliary of the Salvation Army as a "Woman of Dedication". In retirement she helped to train SDSU's student teachers.

Aaron Bruce

Named SDSU's Director of Diversity in 2008, Aaron Bruce arrived here from Rhode Island College where he was director of multicultural affairs. The recipient of a doctorate in education from the University of Rhode Island, he has worked in management positions in companies in Africa and Latin America and has researched management strategies, education and public health in Kenya, Mexico, and Cuba.

Diedrick A. Graham

From 2006 to 2008 Diedrick Graham was SDSU's student ombudsman. Prior to this he was a U.S. Navy chaplain who had served in Operation Iraqi Freedom and had been honored with the Military Chaplains of the Year Award. In 2009 he was promoted from associate ombudsman to ombudsman officer at Princeton University. Graham holds graduate degrees in divinity and human relations.

Jini Hogg-Bornes

Former SDSU All-American 400 meters sprinter Jini Hogg got her master's degree in counseling and for a while worked here in Academic Support Services and at Grossmont College in academic advising before returning to join SDSU's EOP professionals in the spring of 2008. This San Francisco native attended President Barack Obama's 2008 Inauguration along with other Aztec faculty and staff (among them Dr. Shirley Weber, Aaron Bruce, and Dr. Tanis Starck).

Richard Thompson

SDSU Associate Professor of Music Richard Thompson teaches jazz performance, jazz history, and music theory. His undergraduate degree in music is from the University of Edinburgh in Scotland, his native land. Thompson's graduate degree is from Rutgers University where he studied jazz piano and classical piano, and he has a jazz diploma from The Berklee College of Music in Boston. A performer and a composer, he has appeared in live broadcasts of B.B.C. Jazz and Classical Radio and the Italian National Television and Radio. Thompson has played in the Harlem Festival Orchestra, The Boston Orchestra and Chorale, The Glasgow Chamber Orchestra, and more. In 1999 he was the recipient of the first Individual Artist Award from the Brooklyn Arts Council for classical music composition "Legend of the Moors." Other compositions have been performed by the Long Island Sound Symphony Orchestra, and the Manhattan Chamber Orchestra. In 2008 his jazz group, Mirage, released a CD titled "Swing Low, Sweet Chariot."

Atim Otii

Atim Otii A 2002 graduate of SDSU, Atim Otii, was captain of the Aztec Women's basketball team. Born in Denver, Colorado, she received her law degree at Washburn University in Kansas. Otii returned to her home state, was admitted to the Colorado Bar in 2007, and practiced immigration law, specializing in removal/deportation proceedings. The child of a refugee family from Uganda, she has helped African refugees via St. Ignatius Loyola Church; maintained human rights ties and various assistance to Uganda; and was legal volunteer in Gulfport, Mississippi following the catastrophe of Hurricane Katrina.

Akbar Gbaja-Biamila

A football analyst for the local NBC affiliate, the MTN Network, and CBS College Sports Network, Akbar Gbaja graduated from SDSU in 2002 with a degree in communication. He next played professional football with the San Diego Chargers, Oakland Raiders, and Miami Dolphins. To prepare for his transition to broadcast media he completed the NFL Broadcast Boot Camp in Laurel, New Jersey and the NFL Entrepreneurial Management Program at The Wharton Business School, University of Pennsylvania. In 2012 was employed by the NFL Network

Rudolph Allister Johnson III.

Following in the footsteps of his father, Rudolph "Rudy" Johnson III., is also an SDSU alumnus (master's degree in public administration). He is currently President and CEO of the Neighborhood House Association (NHA), having previously been General Manager of the San Diego Convention Center. The NHA employs approximately 1,000 persons, has an annual budget approaching $100 million, operates out of 130 locations, and is best known for its management of Head Start, a program he benefited from as a child. The NHA also provides a senior center, an adult daycare center, a teen pregnancy program, and a HUD counseling program. In 2003, Johnson and his mother, psychotherapist Dr. Lorraine R. Johnson, co-authored the book *Cracking Up: The True Story of One Family's Recovery from the Devastation of Crack Cocaine* (Mosley Publishing).

Shalamon A. Duke

Dr, Shalamon Duke is Dean of Disabled Students Programs & Services at West Los Angeles College. He was formerly Dean of Counseling and Special Programs at Coastline Community College in Fountain Valley, California. He earned his master's in counseling at SDSU (Class of 2000) and his doctorate in educational leadership and community college administration at the University of Southern California. He is a founding member of African American Male Education Network and Development (A2MEND) and is involved with Phi Beta Sigma Fraternity and the National Association of Student Personnel Administrators, among others.

Hamse Warfa

Having fled war-ravaged Somalia at age 16, human rights activist Wamse Warfa eventually landed in San Diego where he attended Crawford High School and SDSU and founded Horn of Africa Studies and Affairs (HASA). He has worked as program officer at Alliance Healthcare Foundation. He pursued a master's degree in organizational management and earned a certificate in conflict analysis and prevention at the United Sates Institute of Peace in Washington, D.C., a place where he frequently traveled to lobby for peaceful alternatives in the Horn of Africa. He was named one of *San Diego Metropolitan Magazine*'s "40 Under 40" persons of distinction in the county. Currently, Warfa is Program Officer at Margaret A. Cargill Philanthropies which is headquartered in Minnesota.

Jamahl Calvin Kersey

Atty. Jamahl Kersey practices tort and business law for the firm of Trachtman & Trachtman in Mission Viejo, California. A 2005 SDSU graduate in Spanish, Kersey received his law degree at the University of San Diego where he distinguished himself on the Mock Trial Team. He was admitted to the bar in 2009. He returned to San Diego to open his own law firm specializing in immigration and criminal defense.

Lynell Hamilton

In 2008, former sociology major and running back for the Aztec football team Lynell Hamilton from Stockton, California, signed with the practice squad of the New Orleans Saints and, though injured at the time, was fortunate to have been on the team's roster when it won the 2010 Super Bowl. When his pro football career ended he returned to SDSU as a graduate assistant

Delroi Estell Whitaker Jr.

Since 2008 Roy Whitaker has lectured in the Religious Studies department while working on his doctoral dissertation at Claremont Graduate University. He received master's degrees at Harvard University and Princeton Theological Seminary. Upon receiving his Ph.D. in 2014 he advanced from lecturer to Assistant Professor of Religious Studies.

Jon Edward Cawthorne

Arriving from the Detroit Public Library in 2002, Jon E. Cawthorne rose from Associate University Librarian to Interim Dean of the University Library in 2008 while simultaneously working on his doctorate at Simmons College Graduate School of Library and Information Science. The son of the well known former local TV news reporter and administrator Herb Cawthorne, he departed SDSU in December 2010 he left to become Associate University Librarian for Public Services at Boston College and in 2014 was became Dean of the Libraries at the West Virginia University.

Jacqueline D. Leak

Cultural psychologist, Dr. "Jacki" Leak earned her undergraduate degree at SDSU and her doctorate at Alliant International University. A 17-year retired New York City police detective, she currently lectures in the psychology department at Cal State-San Marcos and in the Women's Studies department at SDSU. When not in the classroom she is a hypnotherapist in private practice and a life-skills coach.

Lenoar Foster

After receiving three degrees at the University of Nevada-Reno, he did advanced study at Stanford University as a William Coe Fellow in History. Upon leaving his teaching post at SDSU in 2003 he became associate dean for research and graduate studies and, later, interim dean of the College of Education at Washington State University. A former high school principal, at age 57, he died on June 26, 2009.

Latrice Crystal Pichon

After earning her master's degree in public health at SDSU in 2003, Latrice C. Pichon proceeded to acquire her doctorate in the joint SDSU/UC-San Diego program in 2008. She is the principal author of the 2005 article "Ethnoracial Differences Among Outdoor Workers in Key Sun-Safety Behaviors" in the *American Journal of Preventive Medicine*. A postdoctoral Kellogg Health Scholar fellowship at the University of Michigan allowed her to work on an HIV/AIDS education program in Flint, Michigan's African American community. Currently, she is an assistant professor of public health at the University of Memphis.

21ST CENTURY PROFILES

Kawhi Anthony Leonard

20-year-old Kawhi Leonard went 15th in the 2011 NBA draft. Picked by the Indiana Pacers, he was immediately traded to the San Antonio Spurs. A Mountain West Conference tournament MVP and Fox Sports second Team All-American, the Riverside, California native was the Aztec's leading scorer. With the San Antonio Spurs since 2011, in the 2014 NBA Championship finals he was awarded the MVP distinction, scoring 29 points in game three.

SaBrina Bre White

Arriving at SDSU in the year 2000, SaBrina White got her master's degree and doctorate in education at SDSU. She has many years of experience working with student athletes and is Assistant Director of Student-Athlete Academic Support Services, helping the university's athletes stay on course academically and also to give back to the community. She is a member of Alpha Kappa Alpha sorority.

Darius Spearman

With a master's degree in history and a second master's degree from SDSU in education (Class of '06), Darius Spearman has been a professor at San Diego City College since 2007. Prior to his position at the college he was Director of the Intercultural Center at Sonoma State University.

Mary J. Wardell-Ghirarduzzi

Prior to becoming Vice Provost for Diversity, Community Engagement and Outreach at the University of San Francisco, Dr. Mary Wardell-Ghirarduzzzi was Dean of Students there. Her M.A. in cross cultural counseling is from SDSU in 1988 and her Ed.D. is from Pepperdine University.

Chris Robinson

In 2006 Chris Robinson, then Oprah Winfrey's personal trainer, was featured in her magazine, Oxygen. A former SDSU track and field star and graduate in kinesiology, in 2009 he has appeared on "CBS Early Show" and "Martha Stewart Morning Show". His 2008 book is titled *The Core Connection: Go From Fat to Flat by Using Your Abs for a Total Body Workout*. Chris, a certified Pilates instructor who trained under the legendary Romana Kryzanowska, was also twice Muay Thai kickboxing champion.

Nicole Anderson

From 2002 to 2004 Nicole Anderson was an assistant coach of the Aztecs women's basketball team. Previous to this, she was a head coach at San Diego's Francis Parker High School. In 2009 she was picked as head coach of the women's basketball team at Texas A&M University at Commerce.

Tamiko Plashette Nash

Tamiko Nash, an SDSU alum who earned her B.S. degree in child and family development in 2002 was the winner of Miss California USA 2005. She came close to becoming Miss USA in 2006 when allegations of drug and alcohol use were leveled against the then reigning Miss USA (Nash was first runner up). Since her reign the former La Jolla elementary school teacher has worked as an actress and model. She lives in the Los Angeles area with her husband, former NFL player Terrell Davis. She is involved in community and charity activities and is President of The Shine Foundation which focuses on empowering young females.

Tony Gwynn Jr.

Son of the Baseball Hall of Famer of the same name, Anthony Keith Gwynn Jr., has played outfielder on three pro teams: Milwaukee Brewers (2006-2008), San Diego Padres (2009-2010), and Los Angeles (2011-). After graduating from Poway High School he played his college ball at SDSU and in 2003 made the Mountain West Conference All-Star Team with a .359 batting average.

Trimaine Davis

Overcoming a very difficult set of circumstances—drug addicted mother and father both dying soon after his birth---he found success in athletics and came to SDSU to play basketball. An education and Africana Studies major, he was the first student-athlete to be given the Presidential Leadership Award (2006) from the Associated Students. Inspired by his performance on and off the court his basketball coach, Steve Fisher, initiated the Trimaine Leadership Award. Trimaine was outreach, recruitment and admissions officer in Educational Opportunity Program/Ethnic Affairs at SDSU.

Joi Lin Blake

In 2005, Joi Blake, with a master's degree from SDSU in vocation rehabilitation, became President of Palomar College in 2016. She had previously been Dean of Student Development and Matriculation at San Diego Mesa College. In 2011 she successfully defended her doctoral dissertation in educational leadership at SDSU. In 2008 she was awarded an AARA for $400,000 to generate a short-term certificate for mental health workers. Joi also co-developed the African American/Latino Male Leadership Summit which was honored by the League of Innovation for Community Colleges.

Michael A. Goodman

Master Sergeant Michael A. Goodman arrived at SDSU in 2008 as the Senior Military Instructor in the Army ROTC program. He started his military career as a mechanic but later switched to the infantry and became a Bradley Gunner and Dismount Squad Leader. After service in Kuwait he distinguished himself as an Army recruiter and next fought in Operation Iraqi Freedom. Prior to teaching at SDSU he was in Alexandria, Virginia, where he was Research Development Test and Evaluations NCO in the Army's Test and Evaluations Command.

Gloria Lockman Rhodes

Since 2002 Gloria Rhodes (M.S., North Carolina Central University) has been SDSU's Outreach Librarian charged with realizing the library's mission of informing and bringing into its facilities current and prospective students and faculty who need to know about services which impact distant learner, athletes, student affairs and academic support staff, and chronically underserved socio-cultural, ethnic minority, and economically disadvantaged groups. She has made presentations at professional conferences held in Baton Rouge, Orlando, San Francisco, Houston, Denver, and Atlanta. Gloria has chaired the Racial and Ethnic Diversity Committee of the Association of College and Research Libraries (ACRL). She spent a sabbatical year researching and interviewing many prominent individuals in the city's African American community, laying the groundwork for future exploration.

Marilisa C. Navarro

After completing her master's degree in sociology at SDSU (Class of '08) where she briefly taught, Marilisa Navarro earned her Ph.D. in Ethnic Studies at UC-San Diego in 2011. Her dissertation dealt with vegans of color in San Diego and their response to issues pertaining to "food justice."

Keishia Baker

Although CHHS graduate student Keishia Baker did not run in the medal round of the 4x400 relay at the 2012 Olympics in London, her participation in a qualifying round allowed her to be awarded a team gold medal. A six-time All-American at Oregon State University, Keisha commuted to Los Angeles to train with her coach. At SDSU, she studies for a joint master's degree in public health and social work. In her home town of Fairfield, California, she co-founded the organization Save Our Student Athletes (SOSA) that encourages after school athletic events.

KaMala Syretta Thomas

Psychology professor KaMala Thomas got her doctorate through the joint program of SDSU and UC-San Diego in 2007. She has taught at Pitzer College in Claremont, California since 2009. Thomas has published her research in *Biological Psychology*, *Psychosomatics*, *Health Psychology*, *Journal of Behavioral Medicine*, and *Archives of Internal Medicine*.

Mitchell L. Hamilton

After acquiring his bachelor's degree in marketing at SDSU, Mitchell "Mitch" Hamilton (Class of '02) got his MBA at Clark Atlanta University and in 2006. He pursued the doctorate in marketing at Syracuse University which he obtained in 2012, the same year he began teaching in the College of Business Administration at Loyola Marymount University in Los Angeles. Dr. Hamilton's research specialty is consumer self-image and brand evaluation in a digital context.

21ST CENTURY PROFILES

Raymond Alexander Thomas

After graduating with distinction from SDSU, double-majoring in business management and political science, Raymond Thomas (Class of '06) was later awarded his law degree at the University of the Pacific, where he was a standout student. He was subsequently admitted to the California Bar in 2010. After working in the Sacramento Public Defenders Office he joined the Vincent Hurley Law Office in Aptos, California.

Tyler Christian Campbell

A diagnosis of muscular sclerosis his senior year did not destroy the spirit of Tyler Campbell Class of '08), the son of pro football legend Earl Campbell. The aspiring Aztec running back had hoped for a pro football career but instead regrouped and finished his degree in business management and became an "ambassador" for the National MS Society. "I view my MS diagnosis as a blessing" he asserted. "I now have the opportunity to share my experience to help others living with this disease and make an impact on the MS community."

Temesgen Garoma

Employed at SDSU since 2007, Temesgen Garoma is Associate Professor of Civil, Construction, and Environment Engineering and he is also his department's graduate advisor. A registered engineer, Dr. Garoma received his bachelor's degree from Addis Abba University, his master's from the University of Hanover (Germany), and his Ph.D. in environmental engineering via SDSU/UC-San Diego in 2004. His research has been published in *Chemosphere*, *Journal of Environmental Engineering*, *Journal of Hazardous Materials*, et al.

Michael Huly Davis

Originally from Orange County, Michael Davis (Class of '07) concentrated on political science and economics at SDSU. He also worked part-time in a small real estate office where he observed the practice of corporate law. This prompted him to seek out a law school to attend and in 2011 he finished the University of Southern California Gould School of Law. Davis passed the bar exam and today is an associate attorney in the huge law firm of Gibson, Dunn & Crutcher, Los Angeles office.

Whitney Ashley

A two-time All-American at Cerritos College, Whitney Ashley, from Moreno Valley, became the first Aztec in 25 years to win a National Collegiate Athletic Association (NCAA) championship. On June 6, 2012, Ashley, a media studies major, won the NCAA women's discus competition with a throw of 196 feet 10 inches which was a Mountain West Conference record and good enough to advance her to the U.S. Olympics Trials. She was runner up in the 2013 USA Outdoors Discus event.

Porsha R. Johnson

Since 2008 Atty. Porsha R. Johnson (Class of '04) has handled personal injury, construction defect and accident, labor law, and premises liability workload in the firm of Cornell Grace, P.C. Prior to this she was a staff attorney with the New York City Law Department where she was promoted to its Special Federal Litigation Division. She earned her law degree at Texas Southern University's Thurgood Marshall School of Law, a predominantly black institution in Houston. At the law school she was executive editor of the Thurgood Marshall Law Review and a member of Phi Alpha Delta law fraternity.

Zachary Scott

Recipient of the Outstanding Student Award at SDSU in 2007, Zachary Scott was also the recipient of the Ben and Rita Stormes Memorial Scholarship at Duke University School of Law, 2008 to 2011, where he was executive editor of the *Duke Environmental Law and Policy Forum*. He previously worked as an account representative for a multinational media company and as a law clerk for a large health insurance company. Today he is an associate in the San Francisco firm of Littler Mendelson, Zac specializing in labor and employment law.

Joei Waldron

Joei Waldron had distinguished himself as a choreographer in Southern California. In 2002 he founded Axxiom, a dance company started at San Diego City College, and in 2011 Axxiom 2 based in Los Angeles. Mainly oriented to hip hop and modern dance, his company has performed at venues throughout San Diego and also in Los Angeles, Arizona, Scotland,

and Spain. With an undergraduate degree from Salisbury College and a master's degree from SDSU, he is employed as an instructor of dance at Palomar College.

Beverly Warren

With a degree in Spanish from Fisk University, Beverly Warren, whose parents are from Guyana, taught English to Spanish speaking students in Santo Domingo and later was Outreach Coordinator at Palomar College through the TRiO Educational Opportunity Center of North County. Her graduate degree from SDSU enabled her to become an admissions counselor and in 2013 she was made Director of Educational opportunity Program/Ethnic Affairs ((EOP).

Antwanisha Alameen-Shavers

Upon acquiring her doctorate at Temple University in 2013, Antwanisha Alameen-Shavers returned to SDSU's Department of Africana Studies, where she had majored and earned her undergraduate degree, but this time as an assistant professor. Her academic focus is African women, black women in liberation movements, black gender relations and female embodiment.

Stacie Terry

In the spring of 2013 Stacie Terry was named head coach of SDSU's Women's Basketball Team. It was another milestone for the 36-year-old native San Diegan and graduate of El Capitan High School who has had previous successful stints as assistant coach at the University of Louisville, University of Dayton, University of Illinois, UCLA, and LSU. Terry, who has a bachelor's degree in broadcast journalism from the University of Texas at Arlington, played basketball at her alma mater and briefly played professionally in Poland in the European Pro League.

Johnathan Luke Wood

Arriving at SDSU in 2011 with a doctorate in education from Arizona State University, J. Luke Wood is the founder and past-editor of the *Journal of African American Males in Education* and has held chairmanships of committees concerned with minority race educational success in the American Association Research Association and the Association for the Study of Higher Education. He has authored dozens of scholarly publications, co-authored two textbooks and co-edited two books. An assistant professor in the Department of Administration, Rehabilitation, and Postsecondary Education, his latest recognition is the 2013 Barbara Townsend Emerging Scholar Award from the Council for the Study of Community Colleges.

Fiyinfoluwa Ani

Anesthesiologist Dr. Fiyinfoluwa "Folu" Ani was born in Nigeria and arrived in the United States at age 14 to live with relatives in Inglewood, California. At SDSU he was involved in community service, sports, and student groups. Among other recognitions, he was he the 2010 Outstanding Graduating Senior in the College of Sciences. He earned his medical doctorate at the University of California at Irvine School of Medicine where today he trains as a resident.

Helen Virinia Griffith

In addition to having coached and mentored local school principals for more than two decades, Dr. Helen Griffith (Ed.D., Class of '12) has opened three new schools in San Diego, including e3 Civic High, a STEAM charter school the San Diego Central (downtown) Library and which she serves as executive director. She has described her proudest achievement as having walked in the footsteps of her grandmother, a teacher in the Deep South, and her mother, a former principal in the San Diego Unified School District.

Jason Aaron Whooper

As an SDSU undergraduate majoring in political science attorney Jason Whooper went abroad to study at Oxford University in England. He later earned his MBA at SDSU, his law degree at the California Western School of Law, and in 2011 opened his private law practice. He has been a panelist on the City of San Diego Commission for Arts and Culture and has sat of the Board of Trustees of the nonprofit theater Mo'olelo Performing Arts Company.

Antionette Jones Marbray

In 2015, Antionette Marbray became an associate vice president in the Division of Student Affairs. She had previously worked here as director of the Center for Student Rights & Responsibilities, and has also had legal posts at the University of San Diego, Bowie State University in Maryland, and the University of Florida. Her law degree was obtained at Duke University.

Tonya Saheli

Owner of Saheli Meditation in San Ramon and Pleasantson, California, is Tonya Saheli (Class of '05) who earned her bachelor's degree in biology at the University of San Francisco, master's degree in regulatory science at SDSU (Class of '05), and law degree at the John F. Kennedy School of Law in San Francisco. Familiar with patent infringement and other legal matters, she has taught law related courses at three institutions of higher learning. The spouse of a minister, she is author of the book *Memoirs of a Young Millennium Preacher's Wife*.

Gemechu Abraham

The 2015 SDSU Honorary Homecoming Chair was Gemechu Abraham (Class of '11), a former player on the soccer team who grew up in Oregon but was born in a village in Ethiopia. After returning from a visit with family in Africa where he delivered donated books to a humble schoolhouse his uncle built, he helped raise funds to bring solar-powered lanterns to the village of Simbo which he personally delivered. Later, with assistance of business and engineering students working in conjunction with SDSU's Zahn Innovation Center, he witnessed the development of a low-cost, human-powered threshing machine that greatly reduced the labor involved in processing teff, the staple food grain of the region. Thanks to generous funding won through competition, supporters of W.E. Do Good, founded by Gemechu, hopes to use the invention to reduce poverty across the nation.

Marcus Bush

In 2013, Marcus Bush (Class of '10), a product of SDSU's Compact for Success program, became chair of the National City Planning Commission, and at age 26 its youngest leader ever. Fascinated with the computer video game SimCity since childhood, he is employed as a city planner at Rick Engineering Company and Moony Planning Collaborative. He is a board member of the National City Chamber of Commerce and the San Diego chapter of the American Planning Association; a member of the Urban Land Institute and the San Diego Housing Federation; for two years was a National City Civil Service commissioner; and in 2015 was president-elect of the National City Rotary Club.

Corey O. Strong

A native of Memphis, Tennessee, Corey Strong graduated from the U.S. Naval Academy (Annapolis) in 2003 and spent eight years on active duty serving aboard three ships deployed in the Persian Gulf and South America, and also on the ground in Kabul, Afghanistan assisting Operation Enduring Freedom. After acquiring his MBA at SDSU in 2010 he obtained his law degree at the University of Memphis and worked in the firm of Wyatt; Tarrant & Combs, LLC; launched the business venture Tabular Rosa Memphis; and continues to serves as a Navy reservist with the rank of Lieutenant Commander. An activist for voting rights, he is a member of the Shelby County Democratic Party Executive Committee and other progressive political groups.

Eyitayo S.O. Fakunie

Earning a master's degree in public health from SDSU in 2016, Eyitayo Fakunie had already acquired her Ph.D. in molecular biology/analytical chemistry at the University of Arkansas, and had done a two-year post-doc at the Scripps Research Institute with the assistance of a Bill and Melinda Gates Foundation grant. She has been an entrepreneur in the field of stem cell research and is currently Medical Science Liaison at Vericel Corporation in Phoenix, Arizona.

Natneal Berhe

Playing safety and on special teams for the New York Giants since 2014 (5th round draft choice) is Natneal "Nat" Berhe, the first Eritrean-American in the National Football League. He grew up with his brother in Colton---their mother African American and their father, the owner of a gas station, who emigrated from Eritrea in 1970. When away from work he enjoys cycling.

Zaneta Owens

2009 business management graduate Zaneta Owens is a high quality leather handbag designer and is the owner of Zaneta Owens Collection, a business she launched in 2013 after she and a fellow student took a class here on entrepreneurship. "Made in California" appears on her gold Zaneta Owens logo, currently being sold online at Finezza Fine Gifts, with plans to expand into the Los Angeles and San Francisco markets.

21ST CENTURY PROFILES

J. Nikol Beckham

An assistant professor of communication studies at Randolph College in Lynchburg, Virginia, SDSU graduate J. Nikol Beckham acquired her Ph.D. at the University of North Carolina at Capel Hill. She had previously taught at Grossmont College, Miramar College, and Piedmont Virginia Community College.

Kamilah Ahsonti Sanford

Orthodontist Kamilah A. Sanford was a biology graduate of SDSU who pursued her dentistry degree (D.D.S.) at the University of California at San Francisco and her certificate in orthodontics at Jacksonville University School of Orthodontics in Jacksonville, Florida. Her pastimes are traveling and horseback riding.

Derrick Jefferson

At SDSU Derrick Jefferson majored in creative writing, then studied film at the Art Center College of Design in Pasadena before earning his graduate degree in library and information sciences at Louisiana State University, in the state where he did post-Katrina volunteer work to restore damaged libraries. As Communications Librarian at American University in Washington, DC, in 2015 he was selected as an "Emerging Leader" by the American Library Association.

Evan Franklin

For awhile Army Spec. Evan Franklin majored in sports medicine at SDSU but switched over to philosophy (Class of '07). After graduation he joined the Peace Corps and chose to go to Morocco where he spent three years as a rural health educator but was often mistaken as a Muslim from sub-Saharan Africa. He later worked with AmeriCorps Volunteers and taught in elementary schools be before enlisting in the Army and becoming a healthcare specialist and combat medic, EMT certified.

Donnel Laray Pumphrey

On December 7, 2016, Aztec football star Donnel Pumphrey, rushed for 115 yards in the Las Vegas Bowl to help lead the Aztecs to victory and thus became the most successful running back in NCAA Division I history, eclipsing Ron Dayne, Tony

Dorsett, LaDainian Tomlinson, Ricky Williams, and a host of other greats. At just 5' 9" and 180 pounds, the Las Vegas native achieved 6,405 total yardage during his four years at SDSU.

Bonnie Reddick

Bonnie Reddick is a native of San Diego. She earned her B.A. in Africana Studies, M.A. in English, and Ph.D. in Education. She's an adjunct professor in Africana Studies, teaching freshman writing and literature. Currently, she is the Director of the Black Resource Center.

Mary Taylor

Mary Taylor serves as Director of SDSU Compact for Success and Collaborative Programs within Student Affairs. Compact For Success collaborates with local schools, districts, and community organizations to ensure local students are on the pathway to college admission. Programs currently overseen by her department include the Compact for Success, the Price Scholars Program, and Students With Academic Goals (SWAG). Mary received her Bachelor's degree from UCSD in Sociology, her Master's degree from SDSU in Student Affairs, her certificate in College Admissions Counseling from UCLA and is currently pursuing her Doctorate in Educational Leadership through the Joint Doctoral Program between UCSD and CSU San Marcos. Her research interests include educational equity and access for underrepresented students, college access, success, and completion, and non-profit collaboration with educational institutions.

Sesen Negash

Dr. Sesen Negash is an associate professor in the Counseling and School Psychology Department. She earned her Ph.D in marriage and family therapy (MFT) from Florida State University and her M.S. in child development and family studies with an emphasis is MFT from Purdue University Calumet. Her program of research examines: the interpersonal implications of sexual behaviors (i.e., pornography, cybersex, and sexual/emotional infidelity) on monogamous dating relationships; the health implications of at risk-sexual behaviors for monogamous couples; and romantic relationships among previously incarcerated men and their partners. She is also an Approved AAMFT Clinical Fellow and Supervisor.

Tonika Duren Green

Dr. Tonika Duren Green is a Full Professor at San Diego State University in the Department of Counseling and School Psychology. She received Full Professorship in May 2019 and is currently one of the two only Black woman at SDSU who are Full Professors. Dr. Green was recently named as the Charles Bell Scholar to oversee the university's program to mentor African American freshmen students. She is committed to preparing school psychologists who are multicultural thinkers and actors, who understand how racial, ethnic and sociocultural factors influence student performance. She is the Director and Founder of the African American Mentoring Program (AAMP, 2001) and is devoted to recruiting and mentoring undergraduate and graduate students of African descent. Her research focuses on culturally-affirming school practices that lead to improved outcomes for diverse learners with specific attention to African American students and foster youth. She has been awarded over 3 million dollars in grants to train professionals to improve outcomes for diverse youth and children. Dr. Green's leadership roles have included School Psychology Program Director, Grant Director, University Senator, Diversity Liaison-Inclusion Council, National Association of School Psychologists Minority Recruitment Chair, and ADVANCE Leader. Her mentoring research and commitment to diversity has been recognized by the United States Department of Education, Office of Special Education Programs as best practice.

In 2016, Dr. Green received an Award of Recognition of Outstanding Leadership & Service from the College of Education, for her 15 years of service to African American students and communities. Within the community, Dr. Green has brainstormed solutions to closing the achievement gap alongside representatives of the Concerned Parents Alliance (CPA), Urban League, San Diego United Front, National Association for the Advancement of Colored People (NAACP), and Association of African American Educators (AAAE). She contributed to the efforts of the Leave No African American Child Behind Task Force and College Bound San Diego Educational Component to improve the scores of African American students on mandated high stakes tests and was invited to be a Faculty member for the Academy of the Association of African American Educators (AAAE), an academy for professional development in effectively teaching African American Students. In conjunction with San Diego State University's College of Education and College of Extended Studies to improve classroom teacher effectiveness with African American students. Dr. Green was the recipient of the Martin Luther King, Jr. Unsung Hero Award (Africana Studies Department) for her commitment the African American community. She is a long-standing faculty member at SDSU (18 years) and is committed to improving the experiences of diverse students.

ENDNOTES

1. "Booker T. Washington, Great Leader, Honored," *Normal News*, 9 December 1915.

2. "Versatile Darkies to Come Friday," *The Paper Lantern*, 24 January 1922, 1.

3. Handwritten notations on Henrietta Goodwin's Registrar's student record card, housed in University Archives/Special Collections, at San Diego State University Library, not only indicates courses taken, grades and credits received, but also that, "credential sent to Miss Goodwyn (sic) 836 Central Ave., Los Angeles, September 13, 1913." Another notation revealed that a transcript of Goodwin's academic record was forwarded to her on January 16, 1925 after she became "Mrs. Freeman (of) Redlands, Cal."

4. Details about members of the Goodwin family can be gleaned from enumerated census data. See: Bureau of the Census, *Thirteenth Census of the United States: 1910 Population* (population schedule for San Diego County), C 56.2: T 624/Film reel 94, in the government publications collection of the San Diego State University Library.

5. William Grant Still, *Twelve Negro Spirituals* (New York: Hand Brothers Music Co., 1937).

6. Ruby Berkley Goodwin, *It's Good To Be Black* (Garden City, NY: Doubleday, 1953).

7. Raymond G. Star, *San Diego State University: A History in Word and Image* (San Diego: San Diego State University Press, 1995), 49-69.

8. "Negro Education Will be Subject of Address," *The Aztec*, 29 April 1938, 4. "Negro Education Will be Subject of Address," The Aztec, 29 April 1938, 4.

9. Gail Madyun, "In the Midst of Things: Rebecca Craft and the Woman's Civic League," *Journal of San Diego History* 34 (1988): 33-34.

10. Bessie Cobb, "If I Could Choose," *El Palenque* (spring 1938): 22.

11. Paradine Ruff and Emory J. Tolbert, *From Beacon Light to Thirty-First Street: A Pictorial history of Black Seventh Day Adventists in San Diego* (San Diego?: n.p., 1980?), p. 4.

12. *Los Angeles Sentinel*, 7 July 1949, sec. B, p. 8.

13. Ibid.

14. Bob Falconer, "Handy, Gorham Address Armistice," *The Aztec*, 10 November 1936, 1.

15. *SDSU Report*, May 1988, n.p.

16. David Graham, "He Helped Break Color Barrier at Balboa Course," *San Diego Union-Tribune*, sec. B, p. 2.

17. See: Joseph J. Boris, ed., *Who's Who in Colored America* (New York: Who's Who in Colored America Corp., 1929); and Commodore Wynn, ed., *Negro Who's Who in California* (Los Angeles?: "Negro Who's Who in California" Publishing Co.,1948).

18. "Y Committee Finds Negro Positions Limited," *The Aztec*, 3 June 1941, 4.

19. *The Aztec*, 29 April 1941, fig. (cartoon), 4.

20. Ibid.

21. *Del Sudoeste*, 1942 (San Diego: Associated Students, 1942), fig. (photograph) 167.

22. "Faculty Comment on Race Pamphlet," *The Aztec*, 13 April 1944, 1.

23 "Race Play Wins One-Act Award," *The Aztec*, 4 March 1948, 1.

24 "College Anti-Discrimination Plan Defeated, Count Shows," *San Diego Union*, 2 June 1948, 6.

25 For additional biographical material on Orlando Coons see: Jack Williams, "Orlando Coons, 82; Engineer, Accomplished Gymnast and Coach," *San Diego Union-Tribune*, 12 September 1998, sec. B, p. 13; Janet Sutter, "Learning About Life's Twists, Turns," *San Diego Union*, 17 July 1988, sec. D, p. 2; "Helicopter Engineer," *Ebony*, July 1968, 6; Orlando Coons Jr., "Community Mourns Passing of Master Teacher!," 11 September 1998. http://www.laprensa-sandiego.org/archieve/september11/coons.htm> (2 June 2003).

26 Charles W. Dryden, *A-Train: Memoirs of a Tuskegee Airman* (Tuscaloosa: University of Alabama Press, 1997), 44.

27 William G. Swank and James D. Smith III, "This was Paradise: Voices of the Pacific Coast League Padres," *Journal of San Diego History*, 41 (winter 1995): 26.

28 Ibid., 25.

29 Ibid., 26.

30 Ruby Hubert and Clarice Simon, *A Century of Black Princes: A Family Tree* (California?: R. Hubert and C. Simon, 1985).

31 "Progressive Step," *The Aztec*, 3 February 1949, 2.

32 Robert Fikes Jr., telephone interview by author, San Diego State University, 13 March 2002.

33 "Interfaith Racial Panel to Discuss Minorities," *The Aztec*, 9 May 1952, 5.

34 "Anti-Prejudice Law Passed by Council." *The Aztec*, 2 May 1952, 3.

35 Julius Lester, *All is Well* (New York, Morrow, 1976), 47.

36 Julius Lester, "Frats Use Poor Taste" (in "Letters to the Editor" section), *The Aztec*, 8 May 1959, 4.

37 To date, the most extension article on Dr. Long's career is: Cyril Jones Kellett, "Healing From on High," *The Southern Cross*, 5 April 2001, 24-25.

38 "Dr. Markey Joins SDS Faculty," *The Aztec*, 12 October 1956, 8.

39 David Smollar, "Memories of the Past, Hope for the Future," *Los Angeles Times*, 31 July 1991, San Diego County edition. ProQuest Research Library database (3 June 2003).

40 Lester, *All is Well*, 48.

41 James Cartwright Jr., "San Diego Discrimination Charged," interview by Joe Innis, *The Aztec*, 1 April 1960, 5.

42 Ibid.

43 "Sign Carriers Get Message Across," *San Diego Union*, sec. A. p. 2.

44 "Intolerant Fraternities," *The Aztec*, 16 February 1945, 2.

45 Cathy Pearson, "King Praises Civil Rights Bill; Outlines Three-Point Program," *The Daily Aztec*, 2 June 1964, 9.

46 Welton Jones, "A Stranger in His Own Town," *San Diego Union*, 12 March 1978, E-1.

47 Nancy Morgan, "Dr. Crockett Bitterly Attacks Employment Practices at SDS," *The Daily Aztec*, 10 November 1965, 1.

48 David Smollar, "Memories of the Past, Hope for the Future," *Los Angeles Times* (San Diego County Edition), 31 July 1991, B-1.

ENDNOTES

49 Jose Arballo Jr., "Perris Man Gets Prison in Slaying," *The Press-Enterprise*, 30 July 2003, B-1.

50 Diane Ingalls, "Black Studies Sees Goal," *The Daily Aztec*, 10 November 1972, 1.

51 "BSC Chairman Attacks Aztec on Flack Review," The Daily Aztec, 17 November 1971, 1.

52 Report from OFCCP/ESA Assistant Regional Administrator William Gladden (signed on June 29, 1983 for Gladden by Edgar A. Collins) titled "Notification Of Results of Investigation," page 2, point 5-B (Findings).

53 Letter from Ralph C. Casarez, Director of the Van Nuys Area of OFCCP, to Pres. Thomas B. Day, dated April 26, 1983.

54 *Report of the Fifth Year Accreditation Visit to San Diego State University on 29-31 March 1989 by the Western Association of Schools and Colleges.* Oakland, CA: Western Association of Schools and Colleges, 1989.

55 Robert Richelman, "SDSU Affirmative Action Tries to Remedy Past Discrimination," *Daily Aztec*, 12 October, 1983, 3.

56 Ibid.

57 *A Black Perspective on the Failure of Affirmative Action at San Diego State University: A History and Commentary* (Report #1, Part I). Issued by the Study Commission on Black Affairs and the California Black Faculty and Staff Association, December 1989.

58 *A Black Perspective on the Failure of Affirmative Action at San Diego State University: A History and Commentary* (Report #1, Part I). Issued by the Study Commission on Black Affairs and the California Black Faculty and Staff Association, December 1989.

59 Dana Wilkie, "SDSU Black Leaders, Day Clash Over Hiring," *San Diego Tribune*, 3 February 1990, B-1.

60 "SDSU President Defends Record on Minority Hiring," *San Diego Union*, 3 February 1990, B-3.

61 Ibid.

62 *A Black Perspective on the Status of Affirmation at San Diego State University* (Second Annual Report). Issued by the Study Commission on Black Affairs and the California Black Faculty and Staff Association. May 1991.

63 Tanya Schevitz, "Up From the Depths," *San Francisco Chronicle*, 14 July 2000, A-17.

ADDENDUM A

Selected Publications by Black SDSU Faculty and Staff

Here is a representative sampling of books and articles authored, co-authored, and edited by African American faculty and staff at SDSU, though not necessarily during their employment here. Each person is limited to one book and/or one article for this list. Home departments are in parenthesis.

Books and Monographs

Anderson, E. Frederick (Social Work). *The Development of Leadership and Organization Building in the Black Community in Los Angeles From 1900 Through World War II.* Century Twenty One Pub., 1980.

Blake, James W. (Africana Studies). *Behind the Mask: A Collection of Poems.* J. Richardson, 1974.

Blue, Carroll P. (Film). *The Dawn at My Back: A Memoir of a Black Texas Upbringing.* University of Texas Press, 2003.

Bradley, David H. (English). *The Chaneysville Incident.* Harper & Row, 1981.

Roy L Brooks

Brooks, Roy L. (Africana Studies). *Structures of Judicial Decision-Making From Legal Formalism to Critical Theory.* Carolina Academic Press. 2002.

Brown, John R., "What You Can Do Now," *Today's Education*, 62 (January 1973).

Brown, Tanya (EOP). *The San Diego County Ethnic & Women-Owned Business Directory.* Ethnic Resources Unlimited, 1995.

Butler, David H. (Accounting). *An Income Tax Planning Model for Small Business.* UMI Research Press, 1981.

Cawthorne, Jon E. (Library). "Partnerships and Connections—Integrating Outreach and Building Partnerships—Expanding Our Role in the Learning Community," *College & Research Libraries*, 64 (2003).

Coleman, James W. (English). *Blackness and Modernism: The Literary Career of John Edgar Wideman.* University Press of Mississippi, 1989.

Cornwell, JoAnne J. (French/Africana Studies). *That Hair Thing: And the Sisterlocks Approach.* Sisterlocks Pub., 1997.

Ellis, Arthur, L. (Social Work). *The Black Power Brokers.* Century Twenty One Pub., 1980.

Farmbry, Kyle W. (Public Administration). *The String Bracelet: Reflections of and By the Young People of Southeast Asia.* Intercultural Productions, 1989.

James W. Coleman

Fikes, Robert, Jr. (Library). *Racist & Sexist Quotations.* R & E Research, 1992.

Foster, Frances S. (English). *Written By Herself: Literary Production By African American Women, 1746-1892.* Indiana University Press, 1993.

Foster, Lenoar (Education). *Affirmed Action: Essays on the Academic and Social Lives of White Faculty Members at Historically Back Colleges and Universities.* Rowman & Littlefield, 1999.

THE BLACK IN CRIMSON AND BLACK

DeWan Gibson

Eugene H. Grigsby

Edwin J. Gordon

Titus Haynes

Hope Landrine

Gay, Phillip T. (Sociology). *Modern South Africa.* McGraw-Hill, 2001.

Gibson, DeWan W. (Africana Studies), *The Imperfect Enjoyment: A DeWan Gibson Bachelor's Memoir.* Irc Books, 2009.

Gissendanner, John M. (Afro0American Studies). *Proceedings of the Towson State University Multidisciplinary Conference on Scholarship and Creativity of African Americans, 1995-1996.* Towson State University, 1997.

Gordon, Edwin J. (SDSU Press). *Getting Into College.* Mindblast, Inc. 1982.

Green, Tonika D. (Counseling & School Psychology), "The Impact of Ethnicity, Socioeconomic Status, Language, and Training Program on Teaching Choice among New Teachers in California," *Bilingual Research Journal*, 29 (Fall 2005).

Grigsby, Eugene H. (Africana Studies). *Blacks in Wisconsin: A Statistical Overview.* University of Wisconsin Extension, 1997.

Guthrie, Robert V. (Africana Studies). *Even the Rat Was White: A Historical View of Psychology.* Harper & Row, 1976.

Gwynn, Tony (Baseball), "Collecting More Than Hits," *The Sporting News*, (May 24, 1999).

Hamilton, Ronald N. (Communicative Disorders). *Impact 1980: Telecommunications and Deafness.* National Association of the Deaf, 1980.

Harley, Kasimu-Richard (Student Resource Center). *For the Brothers Who Are Here.* Wind and Rock Press, 1995.

Olita Harris (Social Work). *Training Manual on Case Assessment and Case Planning for Child Welfare Workers.* SDSU, 1983.

Hayes, Floyd W. (Africana Studies). *A Turbulent Voyage: Readings in African American Studies.* Collegiate Press, 1992.

Haynes, Titus (Social Work). *Fundamentalism in Black Storefront Churches.* Vantage. Press, 1978.

James-Ward, Cheryl (2009), "What Every Educator Should Know About No Child Left Behind and the Definition of Proficient," *Education Leadership Review Journal*, 10 (1), 57-66.

Jackson, Maurice (Sociology). *Social Movements: Development, Participation, and Dynamics.* Wadsworth Pub. Co., 1982.

Johnson, Joseph F. (2002), "High-Performing, High-Poverty, Urban Elementary Schools." In B. M. Taylor & P. D. Pearson (Eds.) *Teaching Reading: Effective Schools, Accomplished Teachers.* (89-114). Mahwah, NJ: Laurence Erlbaum Associates, Inc.

James-Ward, Cheryl. *Using Data to Focus Instructional Improvement* (Association for Supervision & Curriculum Development, 2013.

Jones, Woodrow (Political Science). *Health Care Issues in Black America: Policies, Problems, and Prospects.* Greenwood Press, 1987.

Karenga, Maulana (Africana Studies). *Introduction to Black Studies.* Kawaida Publications, 1978.

Kerri, James N. (Africana Studies). *Unwilling Urbanites: The Life Experiences of Canadian Indians In a Prairie City.* University Press of America.

Landrine, Hope (Psychology). *Bringing Cultural Diversity to Feminist Psychology : Theory, Research, and Practice.* American Psychological Association, c1995

ADDENDUM A

Logan, Hope (Social Work). *Adolescents and the Child Welfare System. Text and Cases.* SDSU School of Social Work, 1982.

Lyons-Lawrence, Carolena L. (Information and Decision Systems). *Fundamentals of Computer-Integrated Manufacturing.* Prentice Hall, 1991.

Markey, Beatrice G. (Political Science/Public Administration). *Selected Policy-Decision Cases.* University of Southern California School of Public Administration, 1960.

McFarlin, Annjennette S. (Africana Studies). *Black Congressional Reconstruction Orators and Their Orations.* Scarecrow Press, 1976.

McIntosh, Angela S. (Special Education), "The Effects of Response to Intervention on Literacy Development in Multiple-Language Settings," *Leaning Disability Quarterly*, 30 Summer 2007).

Meadows, Eddie S. (Music). *Bebop to Cool: Context, Ideology, and Musical Identity.* Greenwood Press, 2003.

Merritt, Anta. *Jah is My Light and My Salvation: The Life, Times and Reasonings of Kes Tekle Ab, A Rastafari Elder of the Bobo Shanti Order.* San Diego: Imega Books, 2006.

Miles, E. Walter (Political Science). *Vital Issues of the Constitution.* Houghton Mifflin, 1989.

Nesbitt, Francis N. (Africana Studies). *Race for Sanctions: African Americans against Apartheid, 1946-1994.* Indiana University Press, 2004.

Nwankwo, Nkem (English). *A Song for Fela and Other Poems.* Niger House Pub., 1994.

Olafioye, Tayo Peter (English). *Ubangiji: The Conscience of Eternity.* Malthouse, 2000.

Perkins, Joseph (Journalism). *A Conservative Agenda for Black Americans.* Heritage Foundation, 1978.

Perry, Wilhemina E. (Social Work). *Teaching Sociology: An Annotated Bibliography.* American Sociological Association, 1988.

Smith, J. Qwens (Africana Studies). *The Politics of Social Inequality: A Systematic Comparative Macro-Analysis From the Colonial Period to 1970.* Greenwood Press, 1987.

T.P. Olafioye

Stallings, Clifford (Education). *The Secret is Me: A Study in Contrast.* Western Social Research, 1980.

Stanford, E. Percil (Social Work). *Diversity: New Approaches to Ethnic Minority Aging.* Baywood Pub. Co., 1992.

Thomas, Charles W. (Africana Studies). *Urban and Rural Studies.* Ginn, 1971.

Thomas, Shirley W. (Africana Studies). *Socializing the Black Child to Cope in the 1980s.* ERIC Document ED209409, 1982.

Thompson, Lorenzo (Public Administration). *Fire Protection, Capabilities, and Problems in San Diego County, California.* Institute of public and Urban Affairs (SDSU), 1973.

Tolbert, Emory J. (Africana Studies). *The UNIA and Black Los Angeles: Ideology and Community in the American Garvey Movement.* CAAS/University of California, 1980.

Vails-Weber, Dorothy (Counseling). *Sunrise Seminars, Volume II.* NTL Institute for Applied Behavioral Science, 1985.

Van Brunt, Vida L. (Multicultural Education). Strategies for Effective Curriculum Planning for "Troubled Youth." Strategy: Establishing Rapport. Intern's Guide. Teachers Corps Associates: Resources for CBTE, No. 10. ERIC Document ED095155, 1973.

Wallace, Gloriajean L. (Communicative Disorders). *Adult Aphasia Rehabilitation.* Butterworth-Heinemann, 1986.

Waymon, Carroll W. (Africana Studies). *On Being Black in San Diego: Anytown USA*. W.W. Publications, 1994.

White, Lori S. (Student Affairs). *Higher Education and School Reform*. Jossey-Bass, 1998.

White, Lori S. (Student Affairs). *Higher Education & School Reform*. San Francisco: Jossey-Bass, 1998.

Willis, V. Darlene (Student Affairs). *Empowering Parents: A Guide to Taking Control of Your Child's Education*. Liberation Press, 2006.

Wilson, Carlos G. (Spanish & Portuguese). *Los nietos de Felicidad Dolores*. Ediciones Universal, 1991.

Wood, Jonathan L. *Community Colleges and STEM: Examining Underrepresented Racial and Ethnic Minorities*. New York: Routledge, 2013.

Articles

Adams, James P. (Social Work), "A Case Management Framework for Social Work Practice with Family Caregivers," *Community Alternatives*, 5 (2).

Addo, Theophilus (Information & Decision Systems), "The Effects of Dimensionality in Computer Graphics," *The Journal of Business Communication*, 31 (October 1994).

Adichie, James N. (Statistics), Training Teachers of Statistics in the Developing Countries of Africa: The Nigerian Experience," *ProlCOTSt2*, (1990).

Alfred, Lawrence J. (Biology), "A Chemical Carcinogen, 3-Methylcholantrene Alters T-Cell Functions and Induces T-Suppressor Cells in a Mouse Module System," *Immunology*, 50 (1983).

Atkins, Bobbie J. (Education), "AID: A Continuing Challenge for Rehabilitation Professionals," *American Rehabilitation*, 19 (Fall 1993).

Bell, Charles B. (Mathematics/Biostatisticss), "Inference for Goodness-to-Fit Problem with Nuisance Parameters, Applications in Signal Detection", *Journal of Statistical Planning and Inference*, 9 (3).

Berteaux, John A. (Philosophy), "What are the Limits of Liberal Democratic Ideals in Relation to Overcoming Global Inequality and Injustice?," *Human Rights Review*, (6) July-September 2005.

Beyene, Asfaw (Mechanical Engineering), "Performance Evaluation of Conventional Chiller Systems," *ASHRAE Journal*, 37 (1995).

Blue, Carroll P. (Film/Telecommunication), "Film as Reflection: Family, Self, and Creativity," *Sage*, 7 (Fall 1990).

Booker, Beverly L. (Counselor Education). "Using Technology to Promote Your Guidance and Counseling Program Among Stake Holders," *Professional School Counseling*, 6 (2003).

Branch, Andre J. (Teacher Education), "Increasing the Numbers of Teachers of Color in K-12 Public Schools," *Educational Forum*, 65 (Spring 2001).

Brandon, Regina R. (Special Education), "African American Families in the Special Education Process: Increasing Their Level of Involvement," *Intervention in School and Clinic*, 45 (2009).

Brooks, Roy L. (Africana Studies), "Critical Race Theory and Classical Liberal Civil Rights Scholarship: A Distinction Without a Difference?" *California Law Review*, 82 (1994).

Brown-Cheatham, Michaelanthony (Counseling & School Psychology), "The Rorschach Mutuality of Autonomy Scale in the Assessment of Black Father-Absent Male Children," *Journal of Personality Assessment*, 61 (1993).

Regina Brandon

ADDENDUM A

Brown, John R., "What You Can Do Now," *Today's Education*, 62 (January 1973).

Bryant, Cedric G. (Africana Studies), "Every Goodbye Ain't Gone: The Semiotics of Death, Mourning, and Closural Practice in Toni Morrison's Song of Solomon," *Melus*, 24 (1999).

Butler, David H. (Accounting), "Partnership Formation Under the Temporary Section 752 Regulations: A Reply," *Taxes*, 69 (February 1990).

Butler-Byrd, Nola B. (Counseling & School Psychology), "Working Successfully with Diverse Students and Communities: The Community- Based Block Counselor Preparation Program," *Urban Education*, 41 (July 2006).

Butler, David H. (Accounting), "Partnership Formation Under the Temporary Section 752 Regulations: A Reply," *Taxes*, 69 (February 1990).

Callender, Lucinda (Political Science), "A Focus on Implementing Desegregation Policy," *University of Missouri-Columbia Black Studies Newsletter*, 12 (Fall 1987).

Castle, Evangeline (EOP). "Minority Student Attrition Research: Higher Education's Challenge for Human Resource Development," *Educational Researcher*, 22 (October 1993).

Chizhik, Estella W. (Teacher Education), "A Path to Social Change: Examining Students' Responsibility, Opportunity, and Emotion Toward Social Justice," *Education and Urban Society*, 34 (May 2002).

Coleman, James W. (English), "Charles Johnson's Quest for Black Freedom in Oxherding Tale," *African American Review*, 29 (Winter 1995).

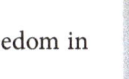

Evangeline Castle

Cawthorne, Jon E. (Library), "The New Library Environment and Information Technology," in *Handbook of Black Librarianship*, Josey, E. J. and Marva L. DeLoach (eds.). Scarecrow Press, 2000.

Estella W. Chizhik

Cornwell, Joanne J. (French/Africana Studies), "Searching for Zora in Alice's Garden: Rites of Passage in Hurston's Their Eyes Were Watching God and Walker's The Third Life of Grange Copeland," in *Alice Walker and Zora Neale Hurston: The Common Bond*, Howard, Lillie P. (ed.). Greenwood Press, 1993.

Curtis, Marvin V. (Africana Studies), "The Lyric of the African-American Spiritual: The Meaning Behind the Words," *Choral Journal*, 37 (August 1996).

Dobbs, Matti F. (Public Administration), "Managing Diversity: Lessons From the Private Sector," *Public Personnel Management*, 3 (1996).

Dual, Peter A. (Public Health), "Universities and Community Health: A National Dialogue for Improving the Quality of Life," *Educational Record*, 76 (Winter 1995).

Ellis, Arthur L. (Social Work), "Urban Youth Economic Enterprise Zones: An Intervention Strategy for Reversing the Gang Crisis in American Cities," *The Urban League Review*, 15 (Winter 1992).

Matti Dobbs

Enwemeka, Chukuka S. (2010). "Blue Light Phototherapy Kills Methycillin Resistant Staphylococcus Aureus". In L. Longo (Ed.), *Proceedings of Laser Florence*, 2009: Vol. 1226.

Farmbry, Kyle (Public Administration). "Institutional Legitimacy Building in a Context of Transition: The South African Land Claims Court," *Public Administration Review*, 65 (2005).

Fikes, Robert, Jr. (Library), "The Persistent Allure of Universality: African-American Authors of White Life Novels, 1845-1945," *Western Journal of Black Studies*, 21 Winter 1997).

Fisher, Delores (Africana Studies). *Readings in African American Music History: Essays*. Linus Publications, 2014.

D. Fisher

Garoma, Tesmegen, "Modeling the Influence of Ethanol on the D. Fisher Adsorption and Desorption of Selected BTEX Compounds on Bentonite and Kaolin, *Journal of Environmental*, 23 (2011).

Gay, Phillip T. (Sociology), "The Moral Minorities: A Self-Report Study of Low-Consensus Deviance," *International Journal of Offender Therapy & Comparative Criminology*, (Spring 1993).

Grant-Henry, Sharon (Education), "Reaction Time, Race, and Racism," *Intelligence*, 11 (October-December 1987).

Green, Louis C. (Economics), "Some Economic Considerations for a Black Separatist State in the United States," *Review of Black Political Economy*, 8 (1978).

Green, Tonika D. (Counseling & School Psychology). "The Impact of Ethnicity, Socioeconomic Status, Language, and Training Program on Teaching Choice Among New Teachers in California," *Bilingual Research Journal*, 29 (Fall 2005).

Greene, Kyra R. (Sociology). "Understanding Racial Polarization on Affirmative Action: The View From Focus Groups." In John David Skrentny (Ed.), *Color Lines: Affirmative Action, Immigration, and Civil Rights Options for America*. Chicago: University of Chicago Press, 2001.

Guthrie, Robert V. (Africana Studies), Review of *Research Direction of Black Psychologists* edited by A. Wade Boykin, *Harvard Educational Review*, 51 (1981).

Gwynn, Tony (Baseball), "Collecting More Than Hits," *The Sporting News*, (May 24, 1999).

Hall, Patrick A. (IVC Library), "Peanuts: A Note on Intercultural Communication," *Journal of Academic Librarianship*, 18 (September 1992).

Hamilton, Ronald N. (Communicative Disorders), "Mediated Career Education at the Maries H. Katzenbach School for the Deaf," *American Annals of the Deaf*, 118 (1973).

Harris, Frank, III. (Education), "The Role of Black Fraternities in the African American Male Undergraduate Experience," in *African American Men in College* (Jossey-Bass, 2006).

Patrick A. Hall

Hayes, Floyd W. (Africana Studies), "The Outsider, Double Vision, and Black Identity: Richard Wright's Desperate Vision." *21st Century Afro Review*. 3 (Fall 1997).

Hughes, Margaret J. (Social Work), "Women, Domestic Violence, and Posttraumatic Stress Disorder," *Family Therapy*, 27 (2000).

Hughes, Marvalene (Counseling & Career Placement), "Holistic Education," *Holistic Education, Journal of Holistic Education*, 13 (October 1985).

Hutchinson, George (Leisure Studies), "The Importance of Recruitment in the 1990s," *College and University*, 63 (Winter 1988).

Jackson, Maurice (Sociology), "An Analysis of Max Weber's Theory of Ethnicity," *Humboldt Journal of Social Relations*, 101 (Fall-Winter 1982-1983).

Ron Johnson

James-Ward, Cheryl, "What Every Educator Should Know About No Child Left Behind and the Definition of Proficient," *Education Leadership Review Journal*, 10 (2009), 57-66.

Johnson, Joseph F., "High-Performing, High-Poverty, Urban Elementary Schools." In B. M. Taylor & P. D. Pearson (Eds.) *Teaching Reading: Effective Schools, Accomplished Teachers*. (89-114). Mahwah, NJ: Laurence Erlbaum Associates, Inc., 2002.

Johnson, Ronn (Education), "Factor Structure and Subtest Differences on the Preschool Behavior Questionnaire in a Latino, African-American, Euro-American, and Asian Preschool Population," *Psychological Reports*, 84 (1999).

ADDENDUM A

Jones, Woodrow, Jr. (Political Science), "Public Policy and the Black Hospital: From Slavery to Segregation to Integration," *Journal of Public Health Policy,* 17 (1996).

Karenga, Maulana (Africana Studies), "African Culture and the Ongoing Quest for Excellence," *The Black Collegian*, 27 (February 1997).

Kassegne, Samuel K. (Mechanical Engineering). "Low-Velocity Impact Dynamic Behavior of Laminated Composite Nonprismatic Folded Plate Structures," *Journal of Engineering Mechanics*, 131 (2005).

Kemp, Helen R. (Chemistry), "Sensitive Sub-Doppler Nonlinear Spectroscopy for Hyperfine Structure Analysis," *Proc. SPIE-Intl. Soc. Opt. Eng. Methods for Ultrasensitive Detection*, 3270 (1998).

Kerri, James N. (Africana Studies), "The Economic Adjustment of Indians in Winnipeg, Canada," *Urban Anthropology*, 1 (1976).

Landrine, Hope. "The Social Class Schizophrenia Relationship: A Different Approach and New Hypotheses," *Journal of Social & Clinical Psychology*, 8 (Fall 1989).

Lyons-Lawrence, Carolena L. (Information & Decision Systems), "My Favorite Assignment: Integrating Writing and Negotiating Skills," *Business Communication Quarterly*, 65 (2002).

Martin, Estralita (Biology), "Bone Mineral Density and Indices of Bone Metabolism in Spinal Cord Injury," *American Journal of Physical Medicine and Rehabilitation*, (Winter 1998).

McFarlin, Annjennette S. (Africana Studies), "Hallie Q. Brown: Black Woman Elocutionist," *Southern Speech Journal*, 46 (1980).

McIntosh, Angela S. (Special Education), "The Effects of Response to Intervention on Literacy Development in Multiple-Language Settings," *Leaning Disability Quarterly*, 30 Summer 2007).

Meadows, Eddie S. (Music), "Hezekiah and the House Rockers", *Ethno-Musicology*. 39 (1995).

Miller, Arianne E. "Whiteness as Pathological Narcissism," *Contemporary Psychoanalysis*, 45 (Winter 2009).

Minifee, Paul A. (Rhetoric & Writing). "Biographical Sketch of Rev. Jermain W. Loguen." In *The World of Frederick Douglass, African American Reference Series*, Vol. 2. London: Oxford University Press (forthcoming).

Neal, Kathryn M. (Library), "Unsung Heroines: African-American Women in Iowa," in *Outside In: African- American History in Iowa*, 1838-2000, edited by Bill Silag and Susan Koch-Bridgeford and Hal Chase. Des Moines: State Historical Society of Iowa, 2001. Des Moines: State Historical Society of Iowa, 2001.

Kathryn Neal

Nesbitt, Francis N. (African Studies), "New Media, Old Struggles: Kat hryn Neal Pan Africanism, Anti-racism and Information Technology," *Critical Arts A Journal of South-North Cultural and Media Studies*, 15 (2001).

Nkwankwo, Nkem (English), "The Artist's Place in Modern African Society," *Ufahamu*, 4 (1973).

Perkins, Joseph (Journalism), "A Pestilence of Lawsuits: Tort Reform Needed to Stop Wheel of Fortune," *San Diego Union Tribune,* (September 18, 1992).

Perry, Wilhelmina E. (Social Work), "Memorias de una vida de obra (Memories of a Life of Work): An Interview With Antonia Pantoja," *Educational Administration Abstracts*, 34 (1999).

Price, Kimala J. (Women's Studies). "Hip-Hop Feminism at the Political Crossroads: Organizing for Reproductive Justice and Beyond." In Gwendolyn D. Pough, et al. (Eds), *Home Girls Make Some Noise: Hip Hop Feminism Anthology*. Mira Loma, CA: Parker Publishing, 2007.

Rhodes, Gloria L. (Library), "Diversity Web Sources in Higher Education Looking at Our Cultural Heritage," *College & Research Libraries News*, 61 (2000).

Samuels, Joseph (Education), "Busing: One Alternative for Some Children," *Contemporary Education*, 44 (October 1972).

Scarborough, Danny L. (Africana Studies), "Black Repertory Theatre: Seattle and San Diego," *Western Journal of Black Studies*, 4 (Summer 1980).

Seaton, Errol R. (Academic Advising), Review of *The Neverending Story* by Michael Ende, San Diego Union Tribune, (October 23, 1983).

Smith, J. Owens (Africana Studies), "The Politics of Income and Education Differences Between Black and West Indians," *Journal of Ethnic Studies*, 2 (1979).

Stanford, E. Percil (Social Work), "Grandfolks in Silhouette," *Generations*, 20 (Spring 1996).

Tolbert, Emory J. (Africana Studies), "Slaves, Workers, and Race Rebels," *Journal of American Ethnic History*, 18 (Fall 1998).

Toombs, Charles P. (Africana Studies), "Black-Gay-Man Chaos in Another Country," in *Re-Viewing James Baldwin: Things Not Seen*. D. Quentin Miller, ed. Temple UP, 2000.

G.L. Wallace

Wallace, Gloriajean L. (Communicative Disorders), "An Inclusive Management Approach for Individuals with Right Hemisphere Deficits," *Seminars in Speech and Language*, 20 (199).

Washington, Patricia Ann (Women's Studies), "Disclosure Patters of Female Sexual Assault Survivors," *Violence & Abuse Abstracts*, 8 (2002).

Waymon, Carroll W. (Afro-American Studies), "Lott and 50 Years of Painful Memories," in the *San Diego Union-Tribune*, (December 29, 2002).

Willis, Winnie O. (Public Health), "Pregnancy Outcome Among Women Exposed to Pesticides Through Work or Residence in an Agricultural Area," *Journal of Occupational Medicine*, 35 (September 1993).

Patricia Washington

Weber, Shirley N. (Africana Studies), "The Need To Be: The Socio-Cultural Significance of Black Language," *Bridges Not Walls: A Book About Interpersonal Communications*, 6th ed, James Steward, ed., McGraw-Hill, 1995.

Wilson, Carlos G. (Spanish & Portuguese), "The Role of the Afro-Latino Writer and the Quincentenary (1492-1992)," *Afro-Hispanic Review,"* 10 (1991).

Wilson, Patricia A. (Public Administration), "A Theory of Power and Politics and Their Effects on Organizational Commitment of Senior Executive Service Members," *Administration & Society*, 31 (1999).

Wood, Jonathan Luke, "Moral Choices: Toward a Conceptual Model of Black Male Moral Development (BMMD)," *Western Journal of Black Studies*, 37 (Spring 2013).

ADDENDUM B

SDSU Awards to African American Faculty, Staff, and Alumni

Monty Alumni Winners

(SDSU Alumni Association award to outstanding alumni)

David Crippens	1973 (and 1987)
Napoleon A. Jones	1975 (and 1984)
Elbert A. Colum	1976
Carl Weathers	1979
Earl Gilliam	1980
Willie Buchanon	1990
Del Anderson	1992
Tony Gwyn	1997
Rulette Armstead	1999
Doris Pichon Givens	2001
Joseph F. Johnson	2003
Leon L Williams	2003
Andre Creese	2007
Cupcake Brown	2008
Fred Norfleet	2010
Joe Fulcher	2012
Harold K. Brown	2012
Christian L. Brown	2013
Amanda J Thomas	2013

Rulette Armstead

Monty Faculty Winners

(SDSU Alumni Association award to outstanding faculty)

E. Percil Stanford (Gerontology)	1986
Olita E. Harris (Social Work)	1993

THE BLACK IN CRIMSON AND BLACK

Arthur L. Ellis (Social Work)	1994
Theophilus B. Addo (Business)	1995
Bobbie J. Atkins (Education)	1995
Winnie O. Willis (Public Health)	2000
Robert Fikes Jr. (Library)	2007

Theophilus B. Addo

Unsung Hero Award

(Africana Studies/SCOBA award to outstanding faculty and staff)

Robert Fikes Jr. (Library)	2004
Sally Mims (Food Service)	2005
Reba Bailey (Registrar's Office)	2006
Estralita Martin (College of Science)	2007
Wanda Clay Majors (EOP)	2008
Charles Neal (EOP)	2008
Donald Coleman (USE Credit Union)	2009
Sandra Bullock (Human Resources)	2010
Tracy Tannihill (Physical Plant)	2011
LaShae Collins (Africana Studies)	2012
Tonika Green (Education)	2013
Maria Butler (Chicana/o Studies)	2014
Michael Mapp (Business Services)	2015
Bessie Watson (Communication)	2016

Tracy Tannihill

Bessie Watson

INDEX

THE EARLY YEARS, 1907-1929

Henrietta Goodwin, 10
Lela Goodwin, 10
Ruby Berkley Goodwin, 10

THE 1930'S

Bessie Alberta Cobb, 16
Blossom Lorraine Van Lowe-Gholston, 16
Clarence Hilayer King Jr., 18
Jonathan T. Buchanan, 17
Robert Clinton Moss, 18
Thelma Gorham Thompson, 17

THE 1940'S

Allison M. Henson Jr., 29
Benjamin Wallace Cloud, 30
George Mitchell Coleman, 31
Harold T. Henson, 29
Ira Lipscomb, 26
John Ritchey, 28
Juanita R.L. Hayes, 31
Olin Lipscomb, 26
Orlando Coons, 26
The Hubert Sisters, 28
Wendell Lipscomb, 26
Willie Samuel Steele, 29

THE 1950'S

Alyce L. Davis, 43
Amos Johnson Jr., 42
August L. Castille, 42
Barbara Louise Anderson, 44
Beatrice Green Markey, 38
Charles Bernard Bell, Jr., 39
Clarence E. Stanfield, 44
Duran Bell, Jr., 41
Earl Ben Gilliam, 39
Edward Sidney Fletcher, 42
Ernest Eugene Hartzog, 43
Evelyn S. Clark, 42
Ferman David McPhatter, 44
George L. Stevens, 40
Grandison Madison Phelps Jr., 45
Harold Kenneth Brown, 37
Homer Floyd Broome, 41
Julius Lester, 36
Julius T. Campbell, 37
Leon L. Williams, 38
Marlene Elizabeth Long, 36
Norvell Freeman Sr., 44
Opalene Carter Mitchel, 42
Richard David Ralston, 41
Robert L. Matthews, 43
Robert Osby, 40
Thomas O. McJunkins, 43
Tony Pinkins, 41
William Glenn Moore, 43

THE 1960'S

Ambrose Jacobs, 53
Andre Henderson, 63
Arthur Joseph Graham, 63
Clarence Stanley Crockett, 55
Claudette Johnson, 62
Cleavon Jake Little, 52
Clifford T. Johnson Jr., 64
David Lee Crippens, 55
Del Marie Neely Anderson, 53
Donald Frederick Shy, 59
E. Walter Miles, 52
Efiong O. Andem, 59
Elbert Alexander Colum, 57
Eric R. Moaney, 57
Ernest Fredrick Anderson, 56
Fannie Lois Jeffries Payne, 61
George W. Pearson, 60

THE BLACK IN CRIMSON AND BLACK

Gwendolyn Patrick-Buie, 58
Haven Moses, 57
Hollis Smith, 63
Houston Robert Ridge, 64
Katye Anderson, 60
Kern Carson, 60
Laurie Lee Center, 61
Leon Henry Osborne, 58
Lillian Kennedy Beam, 58
Maulana Karenga, 54
Maurice Jackson, 60
Mercedes H. Ritchey, 59
Napoleon A. Jones, 54
Otis L. Jones, 62
R. Eunice Aaron, 57
Raymond L. Dorrough, 60
Raymond Quintin Collymore, 59
Robert C. Moss Jr., 63
Roland McFarland, 53
Rudolph Allister Johnson Jr., 62
Shirley Mae Gissendanner, 57
Stephen J. Andrews, 61
Suswyn P. Mills, 55
Taylor A. McKenzie, 58
Tendayi Kumbula, 61
Thomas E. Logans, 56
Thomas E. Logans, 64
Vernon Sukumu, 56
Wayman H. L. Johnson, 58
Wilhelmina Elaine Perry, 56

THE 1970'S

Abdur-Rasheed Muhammad, 84
Alton L. Reynolds, 75
Annjennette Sophie McFarlin, 81
Anthony Keith Gwynn, 72
Arnie Paul Robinson Jr., 75
Arthur Leon Ellis, 71
Carl Weathers, 70
Carolyn Jacobs, 77
Carrol Walter Waymon, 76
Cedric Gael Bryant, 78
Charles Dee Rucker, 87

Charles Kahalifa King, 92
Cheryl Alyece Williams Fisher, 85
Claudie Minor, 86
Clyde W. Oden, 80
Curtis Morning Jr., 78
Danny Lyon Scarborough, 84
Daryl E. Rasuli, 76
David "Smokey" Gaines, 73
DeEtta M. West, 81
Doris F. Givens, 78
Dorothy L. Vails-Weber, 95
E Percil Stanford, 82
Eddie Spencer Meadows, 79
Ellen D. Nash, 82
Emory Joel Tolbert, 76
Errol Roy Seaton, 95
Esther J. Langston, 77
Eugene E. Wigginton, 75
Fahari Jeffers, 72
Felicia D. Washington, 75
Florence Gilkesson, 87
Frances Smith Foster, 72
Fred Norfleet, 74
George Hutchinson, 88
Georgette Katye Bartley, 87
Harold Surratt, 81
Harold V. Rucker, 91
Herman Edwards, 71
Hilton I. Hale, 96
Hodari Adbul-Ali, 93
Hozell C. Francis, 83
Isaac Curtis, 83
James Gordy, 92
James King, 95
James Nwannukwu Kerri, 83
James Princeton Adams, Jr., 82
Jesse Owens Smith, 79
John A. Berteaux, 77
John M. Gissendanner, 87
Johnnie Williams, 93
Joseph Maurice Samuels, 88
Karen Ruth Bass, 94

INDEX

Kasimu-Richard Harley, 81
Kathleen E. Harmon, 92
Keith Mikell, 93
Kevin Edward Chaney, 96
La Verne E. Ragster, 88
Linda Gooden, 93
Louis Cleveland Green, 85
Marian Y. Foster, 76
Marvalene Hughes, 82
Mary E. Cox, 91
Michael G. Johnson, 74
Michele Jacques, 88
Nina Tucker, 90
Nkem Nwankwo, 77
Norman E. Chambers, 86
Olita Elizabeth Dargan, 83
Ollie Matson, 92
Patricia A. Harvard-Hinchberger, 91
Patricia Delores W. Oyeshiku Worthy, 85
Patricia Gordy, 92
Peter H. Henson, 95
Phillip Timothy Gay, 80
Ralph Edward "Mitch" Mitchell, 91
Raymond Crump Howard, 85
Richard Arnold Hill, 79
Robert Andrew "Bobby" Meacham, 89
Robert Fikes, Jr., 78
Robert Lee Wood, 84
Robert Val Guthrie, 86
Roland Wentworth Boniface Bullen, 71
Rulette Villarante Armstead, 83
Sharon Beatrice Grant-Henry, 74
Shirley Nash Weber, 70
Shirley Wade Thomas, 84
Steven Clete Bradford, 90
Steven L. Coons, 90
Sylvia Gayle Dayton Jones, 95
Tayo Peter Olafioye, 87
Terrie Griffith, 75
Terry Price, 94
The Blevins Family, 80
Vallera Johnson, 90

Vernon Oakes, 86
Vinnie Romell Foster-Owens, 79
Walter Kudumu, 89
Walter S. Hawkins, 80
William H. Payne, 77
Willie Buchanon, 74
Willie Edward Hopkins, 89
Willie J. Horton Jr., 94
Woodrow Jones, Jr., 85

THE 1980'S

A. Tobin, 120
Aaron Thigpen, 108
Albert Dwayne Newman, 120
Angela Cranon, 125
Angela Lynn Hudson, 106
Arthur Boyd Jr., 120
Asfaw Beyene, 112
Barron Jodell Peeler, 115
Barron McCall, 104
Bobbie J. Atkins, 105
Cameron Gary, 106
Carmon J. Davis, 125
Carolena L. Lyons-Lawrence, 107
Carroll Parrott Blue, 103
Chana Perry, 115
Charles A. Sippial, Jr., 108
Charles Clifford Shockley, 107
Charles Neal, 105
Chet Carney, 114
Chistopher Karlton Gwynn, 109
Christopher Holden, 120
Clarence Nunn, 119
Dale E. Turner, 122
Daniel E. Walker, 116
Darryl L. White, 107
Darryle J. Grimes, 123
David Bradley, 113
David Harrison Butler, 107
Deidra Hardson, 124
Dennis T. Gibson, 111
Derek Cannon, 110
Derek W. Cotton, 102

THE BLACK IN CRIMSON AND BLACK

Derrick Monroe, 110
Donna Williams, 122
Duke Windsor, 119
Ella Fay Sloan, 108
Ernest Riggins, 109
Ezequiel Fory Palacios, 108
Floyd Windom Hayes, III, 113
Francheska Ahmed-Cawthorne, 112
Gregory Wilson, 121
Henry A. Alvarez III, 116
James Collins, 115
Jane B. Milligan, 108
Janice Eurana Jackson, 117
Jason C.K. Ekwena, 109
Jeff Littlefield, 125
Joan Sabrina Mims-Cox, 106
JoAnne Jenkins Cornwell, 110
Joes Lewis Fulcher, Jr., 118
Joseph Johnson, 116
June Edmonds, 112
Karen Rostodha-Bonner, 113
Keith Houlemard, 124
Kerwin J. Danley, 117
Kevin L. Alston, 123
La Tanya M. Sheffield, 105
Lei-Chala Wilson, 104
Lena Nozizwe Siwundhla, 102
Lloyd G. Cato, 116
Lynor E. Holt Jackson-Marks, 109
Mark A. George, 122
Marsha R. Dodson, 119
Martin Moss, 105
Marvin Vernell Curtis, 103
Max Hunter, 124
Melake Ghebrehiwet, 114
Michael Brunker, 113
Michael D. Robinson, 121
Michael Edward Thomas, 114
Michael Jerome Cage, 102
Millie Robinson, 111
Mshinda Nyofu, 106
Nathaniel Buggs, 121

Nelda F. Farrington, 104
Pamela Elaine Pettit-Noel, 118
Percy Ellis, 112
Perette Godwin, 111
Peter Alfred Dual, 106
Rahn Sheffield, 118
Reginald S. Blaylock, 114
Relda Robertson-Beckley, 115
Richard Lawrence, Jr., 123
Rodney E. Van, 114
Rodney Knox, 117
Rodney Mott, 124
Sha' Givens, 113
Sherma Reavis-Dailey, 125
Shikana Temille Porter, 105
Sophia Angeli Nelson, 110
Stephen Sayles, 118
Susan Love Brown, 104
Taha Taha, 117
Tesfaye W. Leka, 111
Theodore W. O'Neal, 115
Theophilus B.A. Addo, 112
Timothy Duane Shaw, 123
Vincent Edward Mudd, 122
Wanda Clay Majors, 109
Webster Slaughter, 112
William Paden, 121
Winnie O. Willis, 107
Yayesh Lissane, 111

THE 1990'S

Abdi Mohamoud, 146
Adam Russell Jeffers, 152
Allen W. Estes, III., 143
Amanda Jeremiah Thomas, 152
André José Branch, 144
Angela Michelle Byars-Winston, 137
Ashanti H. Hands, 146
Bart Cameron, 133
Brandi Wells, 148
Brenda J. Means, 136
Bryan Greene, 144
Carlos "Cubena" Guillermo Wilson, 132

INDEX

Chanda Nicole Holsey, 139
Charles Phillip Toombs, 134
Chemin Tate, 154
Claire Forrest, 134
Cupcake LyVatt Brown, 130
Cynthia F. Jones, 142
Dawan Percil Stanford, 153
Dempster R. Cherry, 153
Deon Taylor, 147
Desiree Anastacia Byrd, 138
Dwane Brown, 143
Edgar R. Hodge, 137
Edwin Olweny, 149
Emmett G. Shaffer, 151
Estralita Mary Elizabeth Martin, 151
Faith Nation, 143
Felix Goodson, 147
Francine Foster Williams, 137
George Benjamin Brooks, Jr., 131
Grace Hawkins, 141
James A. Raye III, 135
Jarita Charmain Holbrook, 136
John Allen Threadgill, 132
John Arthur Threadgill, 132
John G. Lewis, 150
John P. Hamilton, 150
Juanita Graciela McLean Cole, 139
Kelton L. Clark, 138
Kerry Lynne Hogan-Bean, 139
Kevin B. Winkler, 147
Kim Folsom, 148
Kris Marsh, 148
Kristen M. Howard, 150
La'Roi Damon Glover, 149
LaShanda R. Jones-Corneille, 140
Laura A. Harris, 136
LaVerne Seales Saley, 140
Lawrence Joseph Alfred, 133
Linda Morris Williams, 139
Lloyd Francis, 135
Lorrie Jordan, 135
Marc Carter, 138

Margie N. Spikes, 136
Marlon Farley, 135
Marshall Faulk, 131
Marvin E. Mizell, 137
Matti Fountain Dobbs, 133
Maurice A. Bell, 151
Michael DeWitt Washington, 152
Michael Drew Davis, 144
Michaelanthony Brown-Cheatham, 130
Myrtice Tyler, 141
Nelson B. Robinson, 153
Nola Butler Byrd, 146
Nora Marcella Faine-Sykes, 144
Omo Awo Jahsun Olufemi Ifokolade Edmonds, 138
P. Frank Williams, 145
Pamela Lloyd-Ogoke, 151
Patricia Ann Wilson, 134
Patricia Braswell-Burris, 145
Priese Printz Lamont Board, 148
Regina Malveaux, 147
Renee Swindle, 135
Richard D. Epps, 150
Robert Otis "Grigg" Griffith, 143
Ronda S. Henry-Tillman, 141
Samuel Terrence Waters, 140
Sean Sheppard, 146
Shawn Alexander Ginwright, 133
Shawn Martel Moore, 149
Shouna Shoemake, 137
Stephanie Johnson, 138
Theodosia Ballard, 142
Tia Boatman-Patterson, 149
Tiffany Thomason, 151
Tilisha Tionette Martin, 145
Tony Clark, 141
Tracy Leighton Simmons, 142
Venetta Abdellatif, 142
Victoria A. Love, 136
W. Harold Tuck, 134
Yolanda Pam Gammill, 152

THE BLACK IN CRIMSON AND BLACK

THE 21 ST CENTURY

Aaron Bruce, 170

Aaron Starck, 168

Adisa A. Alkebulan, 163

Akbar Gbaja-Biamila, 172

Andre Todd Creese, 165

Antionette Jones Marbray, 182

Antwanisha Alameen-Shavers, 181

Atim Otii, 172

Beverly Lynn Booker, 168

Beverly Warren, 181

Bonnie Reddick, 186

Brandon Loyvon Heath, 169

Cheryl James-Ward, 167

Chester Pitts, 168

Chris Robinson, 175

Corey O. Strong, 184

Darius Spearman, 175

Darlene V. Willis, 164

Deitre Collins-Parker, 170

Delroi Estell Whitaker Jr., 173

Derrick Jefferson, 185

Diedrick A. Graham, 171

Donnel Laray Pumphrey, 185

Dontia Haynes, 165

Ephriam Salaam, 168

Ethan Neil Kendricks, 163

Evan Franklin, 185

Evette Hornsby-Minor, 166

Eyitayo S.O. Fakunie, 184

Fiyinfoluwa Ani, 182

Frank Harris III., 167

Gemechu Abraham, 183

Gloria Lockman Rhodes, 177

Hamse Warfa, 173

Helen Rochelle Kemp, 162

Helen Virinia Griffith, 182

J. Nikol Beckham, 185

Jacqueline D. Leak, 174

Jamahl Calvin Kersey, 173

James R. Kitchen, 163

Jason Aaron Whooper, 182

Jini Hogg-Bornes, 171

Joei Waldron, 180

John Browning, 164

Johnathan Luke Wood, 181

Johnny Eaddy, 164

Joi Lin Blake, 177

Jon Edward Cawthorne, 174

Juel Ann Giddens Moore, 170

K.D. Aubert, 169

KaMala Syretta Thomas, 178

Kamilah Ahsonti Sanford, 185

Kassim Osgood, 167

Kawhi Anthony Leonard, 175

Keishia Baker, 178

Kristian L. Brown, 164

Kyle Westly Farmbry, 163

Kyra Renea Greene, 168

Latrice Crystal Pichon, 174

Lauralyn Electra Miles Electra Cooke, 162

Lenoar Foster, 174

Lori S. White, 166

Lynell Hamilton, 173

Marcus Bush, 183

Marcus Demps, 167

Marilisa C. Navarro, 178

Mary J. Wardell-Ghirarduzzi, 175

Mary Taylor, 186

Michael A. Goodman, 177

Michael Huly Davis, 179

INDEX

Mitchell L. Hamilton, 178

Naomi M. Hall-Byers, 169

Natneal Berhe, 184

Nicole Anderson, 176

Otis Lawrence Stitt III., 164

Porsha R. Johnson, 180

Priscilla Ocen, 166

Raymond Alexander Thomas, 179

Richard Douglas Hector, 162

Richard Thompson, 171

Rudolph Allister Johnson III., 172

SaBrina Bre White, 175

Sahra Abdi, 166

Samuel Kinde Kassenge, 165

Sesen Negash, 186

Shalamon A. Duke, 172

Sinead Natasha Younge, 165

Stacie Terry, 181

Steven C. Collins, 169

Tamiko Plashette Nash, 176

Tanis Starck, 168

Temesgen Garoma, 179

Terry Warren Johnson, 162

Ticey L. Hosley, 170

Tonika Duren Green, 187

Tony Gwynn Jr., 176

Tonya Saheli, 183

Traci D. Howard, 170

Trimaine Davis, 176

Tyler Christian Campbell, 179

Whitney Ashley, 180

William Demps, 167

Zachary Scott, 180

Zaneta Owens, 184